AIR FRYER
DELIGHTS

AIR FRYER DELIGHTS

100 Delicious Recipes for Quick-and-Easy Treats from Donuts to Desserts

TERESA FINNEY

Published by:
ULYSSES PRESS
PO Box 3440
Berkeley, CA 94703
www.ulyssespress.com

ISBN: 978-1-61243-758-3
Library of Congress Control Number: 2017952126

Printed in the United States

10 9 8 7 6 5 4 3 2 1

Acquisitions editor: Bridget Thoreson
Managing editor: Claire Chun
Editor: Lauren Harrison
Proofreader: Shayna Keyles
Production: Caety Klingman
Front cover design: Malea Clark-Nicholson
Interior design: what!design @ whatweb.com
Cover photographs from shutterstock.com: fryer © Edu Oliveros; churros © Oliver Huitson; zeppole © Marzia Giacobbe; cookies © FabrikaSimf; fruit tarts © Prostock-studio; cinnamon buns © south_juls; donuts © Melica

NOTE: This book is independently authored and published and no sponsorship or endorsement of this book by, and no affiliation with, any trademarked brands or other products mentioned within is claimed or suggested. All trademarks that appear in ingredient lists and elsewhere in this book belong to their respective owners and are used here for informational purposes only. The author and publisher encourage readers to patronize the quality brands mentioned and pictured in this book.

Contents

PASTRIES 83

COOKIES 107

DONUTS   136

QUICK BREADS, BISCUITS, AND BREAD PUDDINGS   164

INTRODUCTION

Using an air fryer feels a little like baking in a future envisioned and popularized by the 1960s animated sitcom *The Jetsons*. An air fryer is a countertop kitchen appliance that cooks and bakes food using hot air circulation—essentially, it's a futuristic oven. Science and technology are indeed to thank for the invention of air fryer baking. The Maillard reaction, a chemical reaction that occurs when amino acids interact with sugars at very high temperatures, is the science behind the browning and crisping that happens in an air fryer. Anyone is capable of mastering baking with this countertop oven. This cookbook will show you how.

Air fryer baking has basically been one big science experiment. I didn't know which kinds of baked goods would actually work in an air fryer, and part of my job has been adapting my oven recipes for the smaller appliance. That meant a lot of reducing of measurements, since the air fryer I purchased was a bit on the smaller side, coming in at 3 quarts in capacity. This means the cake recipes yield a 6-inch cake. Pies yield 6-inches too, unless otherwise stated. There are 3-inch tart recipes in here, for the smallest of indulgences. All of the recipes are technically small-batch, meaning they will serve up to 12 people. If you're having an intimate gathering and want to impress guests with miniature versions of their favorite baked goods, air fryer desserts will set you on your way.

There seem to be countless air fryer versions on the market to choose from. The one I went with and the one I tested all of these recipes in is a 3-quart Avalon Bay air fryer. It has an LCD touchscreen, which really does make it feel cool and futuristic. The fan that circulates the hot air, which is what cooks and "fries" the food, is barely noticeable, and quiet too. My air fryer came with a small 6-inch cake pan, but I found that I wasn't able to fill it with as much batter as I wanted, so I purchased a 6 x 2-inch aluminum cake pan instead, which worked out very well for me to make air fryer layer cakes. The instruction pamphlet that came with my air fryer urged me to fill my cake pan with only about 10 ounces of cake batter, which fills a 6 x 2-inch cake pan about halfway with batter. I think if we were to fill the cake pan with more than 10 ounces of batter, the tops and edges of the cake would brown long before the middle of the cake had a chance to bake at all. So keep this in mind when filling your cake pans; 10 ounces is the magic number.

Some of the baking tools I used for this book that I urge you to get your hands on for these recipes include:

- one or two 6 x 2-inch cake pans
- a kitchen scale, for weighing batters
- parchment paper
- a stand mixer or hand-held electric mixer, both of which will make your baking life so much easier

- a 1½-inch cookie cutter and a 3-inch donut cutter, for making those perfectly round treats
- about four 4.75-inch tart pans with removable bottoms.

I didn't know what to expect when I began air fryer baking. I wasn't even sure if desserts could really be done in the air fryer in a way that maintained their integrity. But I'm happy to report that some of the best-tasting desserts I've had have come straight from this futuristic appliance. It was a real pleasure to teach myself about air fryer baking, and I hope that the feeling of just having fun in the kitchen has been conveyed through these recipes, and that they evoke the same feeling in you.

CAKES

Air fryer cakes differ little from cakes baked in a traditional oven, except where pan size and bake time are concerned. You will become best friends with a 6-inch cake pan for air fryer cake baking. Depending on the size of your air fryer, you may be able to fit a standard 8- or 9-inch cake pan into the air fryer basket.

I purchased a 3-quart air fryer, which is a bit smaller than the most popular air fryer on the market right now, a Philips-brand 5-quart model. The first step in air fryer cake baking is adapting a cake recipe to work in the air fryer. This meant reducing the ingredient measurements for a standard 8- or 9-inch cake recipe by about half to work in a 6-inch cake. As I was writing and baking my way through this cake chapter, I found myself actually preferring to bake and decorate a 6-inch cake. It's smaller and has less cake, sure, but for baking in the air fryer, a 6-inch cake is ideal.

The smaller measurements for these cakes are fun, in a whimsical way that I usually roll my eyes at. Frosting a 6-inch cake put me, someone who is usually an anxious cake decorator, at ease. I'm confident that you'll feel the same way. One note: These cakes will dome quite a bit, but that's nothing a sharp serrated knife won't fix. Decorate these mini cakes however your heart wishes.

Marble Loaf Cakes

This recipe includes some "plus" measurements—don't let that throw you off. Miniature versions of average-sized baked goods often require unusual-looking measurements, as you'll learn in this cake chapter. These marble loaf cakes are pretty moist and don't really need a frosting or even a drizzle, but a dusting of confectioners' sugar is a great idea.

YIELD: three 5 x 3 x 2-inch loaf cakes **PREP TIME:** 10 minutes
BAKE TIME: 33 minutes

1½ cups all-purpose flour

½ teaspoon baking powder

¼ teaspoon salt

½ cup (1 stick) unsalted butter, softened

½ cup plus 3 tablespoons granulated sugar

2 large eggs plus 1 large egg yolk, at room temperature

½ tablespoon vanilla extract

¾ cup whole milk, at room temperature

¼ cup unsweetened Dutch-process cocoa powder

3 tablespoons hot water

TO MAKE THE CAKES:

1. Preheat your air fryer to its appropriate cake setting, or 350°F.

2. Grease three 5 x 3 x 2-inch loaf cake pans with cooking spray.

3. In a medium bowl, whisk together the flour, baking powder, and salt.

4. In the bowl of a stand mixer fitted with the paddle attachment, cream together the butter and sugar on medium speed until light and fluffy, about 2 minutes.

5. Scraping down the sides of the bowl as needed, add the eggs and egg yolk one at a time. Add the vanilla and mix to combine.

6. On low speed, add one-third of the flour mixture to the batter at a time, alternating with the milk until all of the flour and milk has been added. Make sure to begin and end with the flour, and be mindful to not overmix the batter.

7. In a medium bowl, add the cocoa powder to the hot water.

Whisk until very well incorporated and no lumps remain. Add ¼ cup of the vanilla cake batter to the cocoa powder and hot water mixture. Whisk very well to combine.

8. In each cake pan, spoon 2 or 3 dollops of the vanilla cake batter, followed by 2 or 3 dollops of chocolate cake batter. Do this until each cake pan contains about 10 ounces of cake batter total. Create the marble effect by swirling a butter knife or toothpick through both batters.

9. Bake the cakes one at a time in the air fryer for 11 minutes.

10. Let the cakes cool completely on a cooling rack.

Almond Cake with Apricot Preserves and Toasted Almonds

An almond cake for almond lovers. Apricot preserves add a nice sweetness to this, which would be perfect for bringing to a springtime picnic.

YIELD: one 6-inch round cake   **PREP TIME:** 10 minutes   **COOK TIME:** 13 minutes

CAKE:
½ cup raw almonds

⅔ cup all-purpose flour

1 teaspoon baking powder

¼ teaspoon salt

4 tablespoons (½ stick) unsalted butter, softened

⅓ cup plus 2 tablespoons granulated sugar

¼ teaspoon vanilla extract

¼ teaspoon almond extract

1 large egg, at room temperature

⅓ cup plus 2 tablespoons whole milk, at room temperature

confectioners' sugar, for sprinkling

APRICOT PRESERVE SPREAD:
2½ tablespoons apricot jam or preserves

Splash of water

TO TOAST THE ALMONDS:

1. In a dry skillet set over medium-low heat, add the almonds and stir occasionally to ensure even toasting. This does not take very long; stay near your almonds as they toast or they could burn.

2. Roughly chop the toasted almonds and measure ¼ cup total.

TO MAKE THE CAKE:

1. Preheat air fryer to its appropriate cake setting, or 350°F.

2. Grease a 6-inch cake pan with cooking spray and line the bottom with parchment paper.

3. In a medium bowl, whisk together the flour, baking powder, and salt.

4. In the bowl of a stand mixer fitted with the paddle attachment, cream the butter and sugar together on medium speed until light and fluffy, 1 to 2 minutes.

5. Add the vanilla and almond extracts and egg, and mix just to combine.

6. Add the flour mixture and milk alternately to the bowl, being sure to start and end with the flour. Mix just until combined, being careful not to overmix the batter.

TO MAKE THE APRICOT SPREAD:

1. While the cake is baking, add the preserves and water to a small sauce pan over medium heat.

2. Whisk just until the water has been incorporated and the preserves have thinned, 4 to 5 minutes.

7. Fold half of the chopped toasted almonds into the batter; set the rest aside to be used as decoration.

8. Bake the cake in the air fryer for 13 minutes, or until a toothpick inserted into the center of the cake comes out mostly free of crumbs.

3. Poke holes in the cake with a toothpick while still it's warm, and brush the apricot preserve spread onto the cake.

4. To decorate, sprinkle the cake with confectioners' sugar and more toasted almonds.

Brown Butter Cake
with Toasted Almonds

The key with this cake is to get the brown butter back to a solid state by refrigerating it after browning. After chilling the brown butter for a couple of hours, set it on your kitchen counter to come back to a softened state. After learning the technique, you can use brown butter in this way for multiple cake and cupcake recipes! Brown butter pairs very well with ingredients like white chocolate, stone fruit like apricots and peaches, and, like I used here, almonds. Let your imagination take the driver's seat.

YIELD: one 6-inch round cake   **PREP TIME:** 2 hours, 15 minutes
COOK TIME: 26 minutes

CAKE:
6 tablespoons unsalted butter

½ cup whole almonds

⅔ cup all-purpose flour

1 teaspoon baking powder

¼ teaspoon salt

⅓ cup granulated sugar

2 tablespoons brown sugar

1 large egg, at room temperature

¼ teaspoon almond extract

⅓ cup plus 2 tablespoons whole milk, at room temperature

confectioners' sugar (optional)

TO MAKE THE BROWN BUTTER:

1. Add the butter to a light-colored medium skillet set over medium heat.

2. The butter will begin to melt and foam; just let it do its thing.

3. Whisk the melted butter every now and again to incorporate any of the browned bits that have collected in the bottom of the pan.

4. Around the 5- to 6-minute mark, the browning butter will begin to give off a nutty aroma. Don't let the butter go much further beyond this point—it will burn.

5. After about 6 minutes, the butter is ready to be put into a heat-resistant container and set in the fridge to chill for about two hours, or until it has returned to a solidified state.

6. After chilling, set the solidified brown butter on the kitchen counter to allow it to soften to room temperature.

TO TOAST THE ALMONDS:

1. In a dry skillet set over medium-low heat, add the almonds and stir occasionally to ensure even toasting. This does not take very long; stay near your almonds as they toast.

2. Roughly chop the toasted almonds, measure ¼ cup, and set aside to be used as decoration.

TO MAKE THE CAKE:

1. Preheat your air fryer to its appropriate cake setting, or to 350°F.

2. Grease a 6-inch cake pan with cooking spray and line the bottom with parchment paper.

3. In a medium bowl, whisk together the flour, baking powder, and salt.

4. Add the softened brown butter to the bowl of a stand mixer fitted with the paddle attachment. On medium speed, mix the brown butter until fluffy, about 2 minutes.

5. Add the granulated sugar and brown sugar to the brown butter and cream until fluffy, about 2 more minutes.

6. Crack the egg into the bowl and add the almond extract. Mix to combine.

7. Add the flour mixture to the bowl alternately with the milk, being sure to start and end with the flour, and being mindful to not overmix the batter.

8. Pour the batter into the prepared cake pans, and bake in the air fryer for 13 minutes, or until golden brown and a toothpick inserted into the center comes out mostly free of crumbs.

9. Let cake cool slightly on a cooling rack and dust with confectioners' sugar, if desired.

Cinnamon Loaf Cakes

These cinnamon loaf cakes remind me of the coffee cake—packed with cinnamon, of course—my mom used to make around Christmas. We aren't creaming the butter and sugar in the traditional way here since we're working with melted butter, so there's no real need to dirty your stand mixer for this cake. Simplicity, ease of preparation, and a really tasty cinnamon loaf cake is what we're aiming for.

YIELD: two 5 x 3 x 2-inch loaf cakes **PREP TIME:** 20 minutes
COOK TIME: 36 minutes

FILLING:

¼ cup packed brown sugar

¼ cup granulated sugar

½ tablespoon ground cinnamon

CAKE:

1 cup all-purpose flour

¼ teaspoon baking soda

¼ teaspoon salt

¼ teaspoon baking powder

1 teaspoon ground cinnamon

2 large eggs, at room temperature

¾ cup granulated sugar

½ cup (1 stick) unsalted butter, melted

½ teaspoon vanilla extract

½ cup full-fat sour cream, at room temperature

TO MAKE THE FILLING:

1. Whisk together the brown sugar, granulated sugar, and cinnamon in a small bowl.

TO MAKE THE CAKE:

1. Preheat your air fryer its appropriate cake setting, or 350°F.

2. Grease two 5 x 3 x 2-inch loaf pans with cooking spray.

3. In a medium bowl, whisk together the flour, baking soda, salt, baking powder, and ground cinnamon to combine.

4. In a large bowl, crack the eggs and beat lightly with a fork. Add the melted butter, vanilla, and sour cream to the same bowl and mix well.

5. Add the dry ingredients to the wet ingredients bowl and whisk very well to combine.

6. Spoon about ¼ cup of the cake batter into one of the loaf pans. Do the same for the second loaf pan.

7. Sprinkle the brown sugar filling on the cake batter in each loaf pan, then spoon the last of the cake batter evenly on top of the filling in both pans.

8. Bake one cake at a time for 18 minutes each, or until a toothpick inserted into the center of the cake comes out mostly free of crumbs.

9. Serve the cakes either while still warm or once they've cooled.

Classic Chocolate Layer Cake

A classic chocolate layer cake, with the chocolate flavor dial turned all the way up thanks to the addition of brewed coffee—this recipe hardly even needs an introduction.

YIELD: one 2-layer, 6-inch round cake   **PREP TIME:** 20 minutes
COOK TIME: 28 minutes

CAKE:
¾ cup all-purpose flour

¾ cup granulated sugar

⅓ cup unsweetened Dutch-process cocoa powder

¾ teaspoon baking soda

½ teaspoon baking powder

½ teaspoon salt

1 large egg, at room temperature

⅓ cup plus 1 tablespoon whole milk, at room temperature

⅓ cup warm brewed coffee

1½ teaspoon vegetable oil

1 teaspoon vanilla extract

CHOCOLATE BUTTERCREAM:
2 ounces semisweet milk chocolate, melted

¾ cup (1½ sticks) unsalted butter, softened

2 cups confectioners' sugar

2 tablespoons whole milk

TO MAKE THE CAKE:

1. Preheat air fryer to its appropriate cake setting, or 350°F.

2. Grease two 6-inch cake pans with cooking spray and line the bottoms with parchment paper.

3. In a large bowl, whisk together the flour, sugar, cocoa powder, baking soda, baking powder, and salt to combine.

4. In a 2-cup liquid measuring cup, crack the egg. Next, pour in the milk, brewed coffee, vegetable oil, and vanilla extract. Whisk thoroughly to combine.

5. Pour the egg mixture into the flour mixture and whisk until all lumps have been removed.

6. Divide the batter evenly between the two prepared cake pans and bake one at a time for 14 minutes each, or until a toothpick inserted into the cake comes out mostly free of crumbs.

7. Let the cakes cool completely before frosting.

TO MAKE THE BUTTERCREAM:

1. Over a double-boiler or in the microwave, melt the chocolate.

2. In the bowl of a stand mixer fitted with the paddle attachment, add the butter and confectioners' sugar and mix on medium speed until combined.

3. Pour in the milk and chocolate and mix until very well combined and you've reached your desired frosting consistency.

4. Frost the cake and serve.

Mexican Chocolate Cake with Caramel Buttercream

You could use any ground Mexican pepper for this cake; it depends on your desired heat level. A smoky ground chipotle, for example, would complement the chocolate nicely.

YIELD: one 2-layer, 6-inch round cake **PREP TIME:** 15 minutes
COOK TIME: 35 minutes

CAKE:
¾ cup all-purpose flour

¾ cup granulated sugar

⅓ cup unsweetened Dutch-process cocoa powder

¾ teaspoon baking soda

½ teaspoon baking powder

1 teaspoon ground cinnamon

1 teaspoon chili powder

½ teaspoon salt

1 large egg, at room temperature

⅓ cup plus 1 tablespoon milk, at room temperature

¼ cup warm brewed coffee

1½ teaspoons vegetable oil

1 teaspoon vanilla extract

CARAMEL:
¼ cup water

1 cup granulated sugar

1 teaspoon salt

½ cup plus 2 tablespoons heavy cream

1 tablespoon cold unsalted butter

1 teaspoon vanilla extract

CARAMEL BUTTERCREAM:
6 tablespoons unsalted butter, softened

1½ cups confectioners' sugar

1 tablespoon whole milk

1 teaspoon vanilla extract

2 to 3 tablespoons prepared caramel

½ teaspoon salt

TO MAKE THE CAKE:

1. Preheat air fryer to its appropriate cake setting, or 350°F.

2. Grease two 6-inch cake pans with cooking spray and line the bottoms with parchment paper.

3. In a large bowl, whisk the flour, sugar, cocoa powder, baking soda, baking powder, cinnamon, chili powder, and salt to combine.

4. In a medium bowl, crack in the egg. Next, pour in the milk, brewed coffee, vegetable oil, and vanilla extract. Whisk thoroughly to combine.

5. Pour the egg mixture into the flour mixture and whisk until all lumps have been removed.

6. Divide the batter evenly into the two prepared cake pans and bake one at a time in the air fryer for 14 minutes each, or until a toothpick inserted into the center of the cake comes out mostly free of crumbs.

7. Let the cakes cool completely before frosting and drizzling with caramel.

TO MAKE THE CARAMEL:

1. In a medium saucepan, combine the water, sugar, and salt over medium heat.

2. Whisk the mixture until the syrup comes to a boil.

3. Let the syrup simmer without stirring until it becomes honey-colored, about 6 minutes.

4. Make sure to swirl the syrup every couple of minutes to ensure even caramelization.

5. Continue cooking until the syrup is just beginning to turn a light amber color, another 6 to 7 minutes. Be sure to stay near the saucepan to keep an eye on it; it can go from amber-colored to too dark and too bitter very quickly.

6. Immediately add the cream and reduce the heat to medium-low. Be careful when you add the cream, as the syrup will rise and foam.

7. Stirring constantly with a heat-resistant spatula, simmer until the caramel registers 225°F on a digital thermometer, 2 to 3 minutes.

8. Remove from the heat, whisk in the butter, stir in the vanilla extract, and transfer the caramel to a heat-resistant container.

TO MAKE THE CARAMEL BUTTERCREAM:

1. In the bowl of a stand mixer fitted with the paddle attachment, cream the butter on medium speed until light and fluffy, 1 to 2 minutes.

2. On low speed, add the confectioners' sugar to the bowl ½ cup at a time, mixing well.

3. With the mixer back on medium speed, drizzle in the milk, vanilla extract, and 2 or 3 tablespoons of the caramel.

4. Mix until you've reached your desired buttercream consistency.

5. Stir in the salt.

TO DECORATE THE CAKE:

1. Level off the dome from each layer.

2. Drop a dollop of about half of the caramel buttercream onto the bottom cake layer and spread evenly.

3. Drizzle some of the caramel on top of this layer.

4. Place the second layer on top and frost with the buttercream, drizzling with more caramel if desired.

Spiced Cake with Whipped Cream Filling and Caramel Drizzle

This is a great cake to make not only in the fall when it seems like the "spiced" flavor can be found everywhere, but also throughout the year.

YIELD: one 2-layer, 6-inch round cake   **PREP TIME:** 30 minutes
COOK TIME: 26 minutes

CAKE:
1 cup all-purpose flour

1½ teaspoons baking powder

½ teaspoon salt

¼ teaspoon ground cinnamon

¼ teaspoon ground nutmeg

¼ teaspoon ground allspice

6 tablespoons unsalted butter, softened

½ cup plus 2 tablespoons granulated sugar

1½ teaspoons vanilla extract

1 large egg, at room temperature

½ cup whole milk, at room temperature

CARAMEL DRIZZLE:
¼ cup water

1 cup granulated sugar

1 teaspoon salt

½ cup plus 2 tablespoons heavy cream

1 tablespoon cold unsalted butter

1 teaspoon vanilla extract

WHIPPED CREAM:
⅓ cup cold heavy whipping cream

½ tablespoon granulated sugar

TO MAKE THE CAKE:

1. Preheat your air fryer to its appropriate cake setting, or 350°F.

2. Grease two 6-inch cake pans with cooking spray and line the bottom of each with parchment paper.

3. In a medium bowl, whisk together the flour, baking powder, salt, cinnamon, nutmeg, and allspice just to combine.

4. In the bowl of a stand mixer fitted with the paddle attachment, cream together the butter and sugar on medium speed until light and fluffy, about 2 minutes. Add in the vanilla extract and egg to the

bowl, and mix to incorporate. The batter might look a little curdled at this point—that's okay! It'll come together in the next step.

5. Add the flour mixture and milk alternately to the batter, being sure to begin and end with the flour. Be mindful not to overmix.

6. Pour the cake batter evenly into prepared cake pans and bake one at a time for 13 minutes each, or until a toothpick inserted into the center of the cake comes out mostly free of crumbs.

7. Let the cakes cool completely on a cooling rack before frosting and decorating.

TO MAKE THE CARAMEL DRIZZLE:

1. In a medium saucepan, combine the water, sugar, and salt over medium heat.

2. Whisk the mixture until the syrup comes to a boil.

3. Let the syrup simmer without stirring until it becomes honey-colored, about 6 minutes.

4. Make sure to swirl the syrup every couple of minutes to ensure even caramelization.

5. Continue cooking until the syrup is just beginning to turn a light amber color, another 6 to 7 minutes. Be sure to stay near the saucepan to keep an eye on it; it can go from amber-colored to too dark and too bitter very quickly.

6. Immediately add the cream and reduce heat to medium-low. Be careful when you add the cream, as the syrup will rise and foam.

7. Stirring constantly with a heat-resistant spatula, simmer until caramel registers 225°F on a digital thermometer, 2 to 3 minutes.

8. Remove from the heat, whisk in the butter, stir in the vanilla extract, and transfer the caramel to a heat-resistant container.

TO MAKE THE WHIPPED CREAM:

1. In the bowl of a stand mixer fitted with the whisk attachment, add the heavy cream and sugar.

2. Starting on medium-high speed and gradually increasing to high, beat the cream and sugar until soft peaks form, 6 to 7 minutes.

TO DECORATE:

1. Level off the dome from each cake layer.

2. Place one cake layer onto a cake stand or turntable.

3. Add the whipped cream to the top of this layer, spreading out to cover the surface.

4. Drizzle with caramel sauce.

5. Place the second layer on top and place another dollop of whipped cream on top and spread evenly.

6. Drizzle more of the caramel sauce on top and serve.

Marble Chocolate and Vanilla Cake with Strawberry Buttercream

Make this cake if you have a hankering for Neapolitan flavors. Using melted semisweet chocolate in the cake batter rather than cocoa powder takes it to another level, while the strawberry and vanilla pairing rounds out these fun flavors.

YIELD: one 2-layer, 6-inch cake **PREP TIME:** 20 minutes
COOK TIME: 22 minutes

CAKE:
3 ounces semisweet chocolate, melted and cooled

1½ cups all-purpose flour

½ teaspoon baking powder

¼ teaspoon salt

½ cup (1 stick) unsalted butter, softened

½ cup plus 3 tablespoons granulated sugar

2 large eggs plus 1 large egg yolk, at room temperature

½ tablespoon vanilla extract

¾ cup whole milk, at room temperature

STRAWBERRY BUTTERCREAM:
6 tablespoons unsalted butter, at room temperature

2 cups confectioners' sugar

1½ tablespoons whole milk

1 teaspoon vanilla extract

⅛ teaspoon salt

¼ cup strawberry jam

TO MAKE THE CAKES:

1. Preheat your air fryer to its appropriate cake setting, or 350°F.

2. Place the chocolate in a glass bowl and set over a double-boiler to melt, stirring frequently with a rubber spatula until shiny and smooth. Set aside to cool.

3. Grease two 6-inch cake pans with cooking spray and line the bottoms with parchment paper.

4. In a medium bowl, whisk together the flour, baking powder, and salt.

5. In the bowl of a stand mixer fitted with the paddle attachment, cream together the butter and sugar on medium speed until light and fluffy, about 2 minutes.

6. Scraping down the sides of the bowl as needed, add the eggs and egg yolk one at a time. Add the vanilla and mix to combine.

7. On low speed, add one-third of the flour mixture to the batter at a time, alternating with the milk until all of the flour and milk has been added. Make sure to begin and end with the flour, and be mindful to not overmix the batter.

8. In a medium bowl, combine the reserved melted chocolate and ¼ cup of the vanilla cake batter. Stir very well.

TO MAKE THE BUTTERCREAM:

1. In the bowl of stand mixer fitted with the paddle attachment, cream the butter on medium speed for 1 to 2 minutes.

2. Add the confectioners' sugar to the bowl 1 cup at a time and mix until very well combined.

3. Add the milk, vanilla extract, salt, and strawberry jam and mix until you've reached your desired buttercream consistency.

9. In each cake pan, spoon 2 or 3 dollops of the vanilla cake batter, followed by 2 or 3 dollops of chocolate cake batter. Do this until each cake pan contains about 10 ounces of cake batter total.

10. Bake the cakes one at a time in the air fryer for 11 minutes each, or until a toothpick inserted into the center of the cake comes out mostly free of crumbs.

11. Let cool completely before frosting with buttercream.

4. To frost the cake, slice the domes off each layer and spread about one-third of the buttercream on top of the first layer. Place the second layer on top and spread the remaining buttercream on the top and sides of the cake.

Lime Cake with White Chocolate Buttercream

I had initially thought about using key limes for this layer cake, but settled on the regular Persian variety instead, the limes most widely available in grocery stories. I find Persian limes to be sweeter and less acidic, but if key limes sound like the better deal to you, go for it. If you do decide to go with key limes, please note you will need more than three limes to get 1½ tablespoons zest, as key limes are much smaller in size. (I'd recommend five or six key limes.) Citrus and white chocolate pair well together and are the main flavors in this cake. Swap out limes for lemons, oranges, or even grapefruit!

YIELD: one 2-layer, 6-inch round cake **PREP TIME:** 20 minutes
COOK TIME: 22 minutes

CAKE:
2 cups all-purpose flour

1 teaspoon baking powder

½ teaspoon baking soda

½ teaspoon salt

1 cup granulated sugar

*1½ tablespoons lime zest
(from about 3 limes)*

*½ cup (1 stick) unsalted butter,
at room temperature*

2 large eggs, at room temperature

1 teaspoon vanilla extract

*½ cup full-fat sour cream,
at room temperature*

½ cup freshly squeezed lime juice

WHITE CHOCOLATE BUTTERCREAM:
6 ounces white chocolate, melted

*½ cup (1 stick) unsalted butter,
at room temperature*

2½ cups confectioners' sugar

3 tablespoons heavy cream

½ teaspoon salt

½ teaspoon vanilla extract

TO MAKE THE CAKE:

1. Preheat your air fryer to its appropriate cake setting, or to 350°F.

2. Grease two 6-inch cake pans with cooking spray and line the bottoms with parchment paper.

3. In a small bowl, sift together the flour, baking powder, baking soda, and salt.

4. In the bowl of a stand mixer fitted with the paddle attachment, cream together the sugar, lime zest, and butter on medium speed for 1 to 2 minutes. Scrape the sides of the bowl.

5. Add the eggs one at a time, scraping the bowl after each.

6. Add the vanilla extract, and mix to combine.

7. Add half the sour cream to the egg mixture, then stir in half the flour mixture, add the rest of the sour cream, add the rest of the flour, then finish with the lime juice. Stir until just combined. The batter might look a little curdled, and that's fine.

8. Divide the batter evenly into the prepared cake pans.

9. Bake the cakes in the air fryer one at a time for 11 minutes each, or until a toothpick inserted into the center of the cake comes out mostly free of crumbs.

10. Let cool completely on a cooking rack before frosting.

TO MAKE THE BUTTERCREAM:

1. Place the white chocolate in a glass bowl and set over a double-boiler to melt, stirring frequently with a rubber spatula until shiny and smooth. Set aside to cool completely.

2. In a stand mixer fitted with the paddle attachment, beat the butter on medium speed until light and fluffy, 2 minutes. Scrape the sides of the bowl.

3. Add 2 cups of the confectioners' sugar and mix, scraping down the sides of the bowl as needed.

4. Pour in white chocolate and heavy cream and stir until incorporated.

5. Add the remaining ½ cup of confectioners' sugar, salt, and vanilla extract and mix until you've reached your desired buttercream consistency.

6. To frost the cake, slice the domes off the tops of each layer. Spread about one-third of the buttercream on top of the first layer. Place the second layer on top and spread the remaining buttercream on the top and sides of the cake.

Chocolate Cake with Hazelnut Coffee Glaze

The chocolate and coffee flavor pairing is a classic for good reason. In this cake, we're using a glaze in lieu of a buttercream just to switch it up. Feel free to substitute for your favorite coffee buttercream if you just can't resist, though.

YIELD: one 6-inch round cake   **PREP TIME:** 15 minutes   **COOK TIME:** 14 minutes

CAKE:

⅔ cup all-purpose flour

⅓ cup plus 2 tablespoons granulated sugar

2 tablespoons plus 2 teaspoons unsweetened Dutch-process cocoa powder

1 teaspoon baking powder

¼ teaspoon salt

1 large egg, at room temperature

⅓ cup plus 1 tablespoon buttermilk, at room temperature

2 tablespoons warm brewed coffee

¾ teaspoon vegetable oil

½ teaspoon vanilla extract

HAZELNUT COFFEE GLAZE:

½ cup confectioners' sugar

½ tablespoon cold-brew coffee

½ tablespoon hazelnut coffee creamer

TO MAKE THE CAKE:

1. Preheat your air fryer to its appropriate cake setting, or 350°F.

2. Grease a 6-inch cake pan with cooking spray and line the bottom with parchment paper.

3. In a large bowl, whisk the flour, sugar, cocoa powder, baking powder, and salt to combine.

4. In a 2-cup liquid measuring cup, crack in the egg. Next, pour in the buttermilk, brewed coffee, vegetable oil, and vanilla extract. Whisk thoroughly to combine.

5. Pour the egg mixture into the flour mixture and whisk until all lumps have been removed.

6. Pour the batter into the prepared cake pan and bake in your air fryer for 14 minutes, or until a toothpick inserted into the center of the cake has come out mostly free of crumbs.

TO MAKE THE COFFEE GLAZE:

1. Whisk together the confectioners' sugar, cold-brew coffee, and hazelnut coffee creamer in a medium bowl until smooth and you've reached your desired glaze consistency.

7. Let cool completely on a cooling rack before pouring the glaze over.

2. Set a baking sheet under the cooling rack and drizzle the glaze over the cake, making sure to cover the sides. Serve immediately.

Apple Cake with Amaretto Glaze

I used a Gala apple for this because I love its inherent sweetness. However, Granny Smith apples are legendary for their strength in baking, so feel free to use that instead. Apple and amaretto are flavors that I was somewhat surprised paired so well together. The addition of luscious brown sugar in the glaze makes this cake a winner.

YIELD: one 6-inch round cake **PREP TIME:** 20 minutes **COOK TIME:** 14 minutes

CAKE:
⅔ cup all-purpose flour

½ teaspoon baking soda

½ teaspoon ground cinnamon

¼ teaspoon salt

¼ cup (½ stick) unsalted butter, at room temperature

½ cup granulated sugar

1 large egg, at room temperature

¼ teaspoon vanilla extract

¾ cup peeled, grated apple (about 1 medium apple)

2 tablespoons chopped, toasted walnuts (optional)

AMARETTO GLAZE:
¼ cup brown sugar

2½ tablespoons amaretto liqueur

¼ cup confectioners' sugar

TO MAKE THE CAKE:

1. Preheat your air fryer to its appropriate cake setting, or 350°F.

2. Grease a 6-inch cake pan with cooking spray and line the bottom with parchment paper.

3. In a medium bowl, whisk together the flour, baking soda, cinnamon, and salt until combined.

4. In the bowl of a stand mixer fitted with the paddle attachment, cream together the butter and sugar on medium speed until fluffy, about 2 minutes.

5. Add the egg and mix well. Add the vanilla extract and mix well.

6. Add the dry ingredients into the bowl of the stand mixer and mix well, being mindful to not overmix the batter.

7. Fold the grated apple into the cake batter.

8. Spoon the cake batter into the prepared cake pan and bake

in your air fryer for 14 minutes, or until a toothpick inserted into the center of the cake has come out mostly free of crumbs.

TO MAKE THE AMARETTO GLAZE:

1. In a medium saucepan over medium heat, dissolve the brown sugar and the amaretto, stirring constantly. Reduce the heat to low.

9. Let cake cool slightly before serving. Make the glaze while the cake cools.

2. Add the confectioners' sugar and whisk to combine thoroughly. Drizzle the glaze over the cake, sprinkle the toasted, chopped walnuts on top, if using, and serve.

Vanilla Bean Cake with Orange Buttercream

Orange Creamsicle flavors make this a great cake to enjoy during the warmth of summer. While you can definitely use vanilla extract for this cake, I am here to urge you to opt for the vanilla bean seeds. Not only do the tiny black flecks dot the cake batter in such a pretty way, but the flavor impact of straight vanilla is something to write home about.

YIELD: one 2-layer, 6-inch round cake **PREP TIME:** 15 minutes
COOK TIME: 24 minutes

CAKE:
1¼ cups all-purpose flour

½ teaspoon baking powder

½ teaspoon salt

½ cup (1 stick) unsalted butter, at room temperature

½ cup granulated sugar

¼ cup brown sugar

1 large egg, at room temperature

½ vanilla bean, seeds scraped

2 tablespoons full-fat sour cream, at room temperature

ORANGE BUTTERCREAM:
¾ cup (1½ sticks) unsalted butter, at room temperature

2 cups confectioners' sugar

1 tablespoon orange zest (from 1 small orange)

1 to 2 tablespoons freshly squeezed orange juice

1 tablespoon whole milk

TO MAKE THE CAKE:

1. Preheat your air fryer to its appropriate cake setting, or 350°F.

2. Grease two 6-inch cake pans with cooking spray and line the bottoms with parchment paper.

3. In a medium bowl, whisk together the flour, baking powder, and salt.

4. In the bowl of a stand mixer fitted with the paddle attachment, cream the butter on medium speed until fluffy, 1 to 2 minutes. Add the granulated sugar and brown sugar and continue mixing.

5. Add the egg and mix well, then add the vanilla bean seeds and sour cream.

6. Turn the mixer to low speed, then add the dry ingredients and mix until smooth, being careful not to overmix.

7. Divide the batter between the two prepared cake pans and bake one at a time in the air fryer for 12 minutes each, or until a toothpick inserted into the center of the cake comes out mostly free of crumbs.

8. Let cool completely before frosting.

TO MAKE THE ORANGE BUTTERCREAM:

1. In the bowl of a stand mixer fitted with the paddle attachment, cream the butter on medium speed until fluffy, 1 to 2 minutes.

2. Add the confectioners' sugar 1 cup at a time until thoroughly combined.

3. Add the orange zest, orange juice, and milk, and mix until you've reached your desired buttercream consistency.

4. To frost the cake, slice off the domes from each layer. Spread about one-third of the buttercream on top of the first layer and repeat with the remaining layer. Spread the rest of the buttercream on the sides of the cake and serve.

Pistachio Cake

You will need a food processor to make this pistachio cake. Be extra mindful to not overprocess the pistachios, or they will become a paste, which you do not want. I found processing the pistachios for 30 to 40 seconds is safe. Vanilla bean whipped cream is the only topping you'll need, but nothing should stop you from serving this with a scoop of vanilla ice cream too.

YIELD: one 2-layer, 6-inch cake   **PREP TIME:** 25 minutes
COOK TIME: 22 minutes

VANILLA BEAN WHIPPED CREAM:
1 cup cold heavy cream

½ vanilla bean

2 tablespoons granulated sugar

CAKE:
⅓ cup (about 2.5 ounces) shelled pistachios

½ cup all-purpose flour

1 teaspoon baking powder

½ teaspoon ground allspice

¼ teaspoon salt

¼ cup (½ stick) unsalted butter, at room temperature

½ cup granulated sugar

1 large egg, at room temperature

¼ teaspoon vanilla extract

¼ cup whole milk, at room temperature

1 tablespoon finely grated lemon zest (from 1 to 2 small lemons)

TO MAKE THE VANILLA BEAN WHIPPED CREAM:

1. Place the heavy cream in a small bowl. Scrape the seeds from half a vanilla bean into the bowl and whisk to combine. Discard the vanilla pod.

2. Cover the bowl with plastic wrap and refrigerate for 1 hour.

3. Strain the cream–vanilla bean mixture through a fine-mesh sieve and into the bowl of a stand mixer.

4. Add the sugar to the stand mixer bowl.

5. Attach the whisk to the mixer and whisk, starting on low speed and gradually increasing to high until peaks form, about 6 minutes. Refrigerate until ready to use.

TO MAKE THE CAKE:

1. Preheat your air fryer to its appropriate cake setting, or 350°F.

2. Grease two 6-inch cake pans with cooking spray and line the bottoms with parchment paper.

3. Add the shelled pistachios to a dry skillet set over medium heat. Stirring frequently to prevent burning, toast the nuts until they've given off a toasted aroma, 3 to 5 minutes. Remove from heat and set aside to cool.

4. Pulse the toasted pistachios in a food processor until finely ground, being sure to not overprocess.

5. Add the ground pistachios to a medium bowl, then add the flour, baking powder, allspice, and salt. Whisk to combine.

6. In the bowl of stand mixer fitted with the paddle attachment, cream together the butter and sugar until fluffy on medium speed, 1 to 2 minutes. Add the egg and vanilla extract, and mix well.

7. Reduce the mixer speed to low and add in the ground dry ingredients in alternating batches with the milk, being sure to start and end with the dry ingredients and being mindful to not overmix the batter.

8. Add the lemon zest and mix just until combined.

9. Spread batter evenly between the two prepared cake pans and bake in the air fryer one at a time, for 11 minutes each, or until a toothpick inserted into the center of the cake comes out mostly free of crumbs.

10. Cool the cakes completely on a cooling rack.

11. To frost the cake, slice the domes off each layer. Spread about one-third of the whipped cream on top of bottom layer. Repeat with the top layer, and frost both the top and the sides of the cake.

Funfetti Birthday Cake

I wanted to prove that you can bake a birthday cake in the air fryer, and I have done it. Funfetti cake is classic, of course; I made this a three-layer cake because why not? You're probably baking this for someone's birthday, so go all out. This would be a fun "smash" cake for a kid's birthday party, if the idea of a baby destroying your work sounds good to you. I used AmeriColor Soft Gel Paste Food Color in violet when I tested this cake, but feel free to use whatever color is the birthday star's favorite.

YIELD: one 3-layer, 6-inch round cake **PREP TIME:** 20 minutes
COOK TIME: 33 minutes

CAKE:

1½ cups all-purpose flour

2 teaspoons baking powder

½ teaspoon salt

½ cup (1 stick) unsalted butter, at room temperature

1 cup granulated sugar

2 large eggs, at room temperature

1 teaspoon vanilla extract

¾ cup whole milk, at room temperature

¼ cup rainbow sprinkles

VANILLA BUTTERCREAM:

1½ cups (3 sticks) unsalted butter, room temperature

3 cups confectioners' sugar

1 tablespoon vanilla extract

pinch of salt

gel food coloring (optional)

TO MAKE THE CAKE:

1. Preheat your air fryer to its appropriate cake setting, or 350°F.

2. Grease three 6-inch cake pans with cooking spray and line the bottoms with parchment paper.

3. In a medium bowl, whisk together the flour, baking powder, and salt.

4. In the bowl of a stand mixer fitted with the paddle attachment, cream the butter on medium speed until smooth. Add the sugar and cream until fluffy, an additional 1 to 2 minutes.

5. Reduce the speed to low and add the eggs, one at a time, mixing well after each. Add the vanilla extract.

6. Add the dry ingredients to the bowl of the stand mixer alternately with the milk, being sure to begin and end with the flour. Be mindful to not overmix the batter.

7. Fold in the sprinkles and divide the batter evenly among the three prepared cake pans.

TO MAKE THE BUTTERCREAM:

1. In the bowl of a stand mixer fitted with the paddle attachment, cream the butter on medium speed until smooth.

2. Add the confectioners' sugar 1 cup at a time and mix well.

3. Add the vanilla extract, salt, and your desired amount of gel food coloring, if using, and mix until you've reached your desired buttercream consistency.

8. Bake each cake layer one at a time in the air fryer for 11 minutes each, or until a toothpick inserted into the center of the cake comes out mostly free of crumbs.

9. Let the cakes cool completely on a cooling rack before frosting.

4. To frost the cake, slice the domes off each layer. Spread about one-quarter of the buttercream on top of the first layer and repeat with the second layer. Place the third layer on top, frost the sides of the cake, and serve.

Michelada-Inspired Cake with Lime and Chile Pepper Buttercream

This cake was made into cupcakes in a recipe I did for *Munchies*, Vice.com's food news website. I initially used Negra Modelo in this recipe, but any Mexican beer (like Pacifico) will do. When I developed this for *Munchies*, I used the Mexican seasoning Tajín in the buttercream. Tajín is a spice mixture consisting of salt, lime, and chili—these may seem like peculiar cake flavors! But I hope you'll trust me, and trust the slightly savory flavors that are happening here.

YIELD: one 2-layer, 6-inch cake **PREP TIME:** 25 minutes
COOK TIME: 24 minutes

CAKE:

1¼ cups all-purpose flour

1 teaspoon baking powder

¼ teaspoon salt

½ cup Mexican lager, at room temperature, plus more for brushing cakes

2 tablespoons whole milk, at room temperature

6½ tablespoons unsalted butter, at room temperature

½ cup plus 6 tablespoons granulated sugar

2 large eggs, at room temperature

½ teaspoon vanilla extract

½ teaspoon lime zest

LIME AND CHILE PEPPER BUTTERCREAM:

¾ cup (1½ sticks) unsalted butter, at room temperature

2 to 3 cups confectioners' sugar

2 teaspoons lime zest (from about 2 limes)

½ teaspoon vanilla extract

½ tablespoon chili powder

¼ teaspoon salt

2 tablespoons freshly squeezed lime juice

TO MAKE THE CAKE:

1. Preheat your air fryer to its appropriate cake setting, or 350°F.

2. Grease two 6-inch cake pans with cooking spray and line the bottoms with parchment paper.

3. In a medium bowl, whisk the flour, baking powder, and salt to combine.

4. In a small bowl or measuring cup, whisk the Mexican lager and the milk. Set aside.

5. In the bowl of a stand mixer fitted with the paddle attachment, cream the butter and sugar on medium speed until light and fluffy, about 2 minutes.

6. Add the eggs, one at a time, being sure to scrape the bowl after each addition.

7. Mix in the vanilla extract and lime zest until combined.

8. Alternate adding the flour mixture and the beer mixture to the bowl on low speed, being sure to begin and end with the flour. Be mindful not to overmix the batter.

9. Divide the batter between the two prepared cake pans and bake one at a time in your air fryer for 12 minutes each, or until a toothpick inserted into the center of the cake comes out mostly free of crumbs.

10. Poke a few holes in each cake layer, then brush the tops with room-temperature Mexican lager.

11. Let cakes cool completely on a cooling rack before frosting.

TO MAKE THE BUTTERCREAM:

1. In the bowl of a stand mixer fitted with the paddle attachment, cream the butter on medium speed until fluffy, about 2 minutes.

2. Add the confectioners' sugar and lime zest. Mix until combined.

3. Add the vanilla extract, chili powder, salt, and lime juice. Mix until you've reached your desired buttercream consistency.

4. To frost the cake, slice the domes off each layer. Spread about one-third of the whipped cream on top of bottom layer. Repeat with the top layer, and frost both the top and the sides of the cake.

Mixed Berry Vanilla Cake

I used a mixture of fresh raspberries, strawberries, and blackberries for this cake, but frozen fruit works too! Just be mindful to follow the instructions on the bag for thawing the fruit.

YIELD: one 2-layer, 6-inch cake **PREP TIME:** 15 minutes
COOK TIME: 26 minutes

MIXED BERRY PUREE:
½ cup fresh or frozen raspberries

½ cup sliced fresh or frozen strawberries, sliced

⅓ cup fresh or frozen blackberries

¼ to ⅓ cup granulated sugar

1 tablespoon freshly squeezed lemon juice

CAKE:
1¼ cups all-purpose flour

2 teaspoons baking powder

6 tablespoons unsalted butter, at room temperature

¾ cup granulated sugar

6 tablespoons full-fat sour cream, at room temperature

1 teaspoon vanilla extract

3 large egg whites, at room temperature

6 tablespoons whole milk, at room temperature

VANILLA WHIPPED CREAM:
½ cup cold heavy cream

1 tablespoon granulated sugar

1 teaspoon vanilla extract

TO MAKE THE MIXED BERRY PUREE:

1. In a medium saucepan over medium heat, bring the raspberries, strawberries, blackberries, sugar, and lemon juice to a simmer until the sugar has dissolved, about 8 to 10 minutes.

2. Remove from the heat and let cool for 5 to 10 minutes until proceeding.

3. Puree the mixture in a food processor or blender. Pour mixture through a sieve to strain any seeds from the berries. Set aside while the cake batter is prepared.

TO MAKE THE CAKE:

1. Preheat your air fryer to its appropriate cake setting, or 350°F.

2. Grease two 6-inch cake pans with cooking spray and line the bottoms with parchment paper.

3. In a small bowl, whisk together the flour and baking powder.

4. In the bowl of a stand mixer fitted with the paddle attachment, cream together the butter and sugar on medium speed until light and fluffy, about 2 minutes.

5. Mix in the sour cream and vanilla extract to combine. Next, mix the egg whites one at a time. Combine well.

6. Mix the dry ingredients and the milk into the batter in alternating batches, being mindful not to overmix.

7. Divide the batter between the two prepared cake pans and bake one at a time for 13 minutes each, or until a toothpick inserted into the center of the cake comes out mostly free of crumbs.

8. Using a toothpick, poke holes into the cake layers and brush the tops with the mixed berry puree. Set aside while the whipped cream is being prepared.

TO MAKE THE WHIPPED CREAM:

1. In the bowl of a stand mixer fitted with the whisk attachment, add the heavy cream and sugar.

2. Starting on medium-high speed and gradually increasing to high, beat the cream and sugar until soft peaks form, 6 to 7 minutes. Stir in the vanilla extract.

3. To frost the cake, slice the domes off each layer. Spread about one-third of the whipped cream on top of bottom layer. Repeat with the top layer, and frost both the top and the sides of the cake.

Paloma Grapefruit Loaf Cake

This is a fun loaf cake to make if you happen to have tequila laying around. I'm a big fan of the Paloma cocktail, from which this cake was inspired. You'll need a food processor to make it. Blending the grapefruit zest with the sugar allows the oils in the citrus to be released into the sugar. (Essentially, you're creating grapefruit sugar.) Grapefruit cake flavors and a hint of tequila—or more, if you're really in the mood to party—in the glaze? I can't see anything wrong with that.

YIELD: two 5 x 3 x 2-inch loaf cakes   **PREP TIME:** 15 minutes
COOK TIME: 28 minutes

CAKE:
½ cup granulated sugar

1 heaping tablespoon grapefruit zest (from about ½ large grapefruit)

1¼ cups all-purpose flour

¼ teaspoon salt

1 teaspoon baking powder

1 large egg, at room temperature

1 tablespoon freshly-squeezed grapefruit juice

½ tablespoon vanilla extract

¼ cup vegetable oil

½ cup full-fat sour cream, at room temperature

TEQUILA GLAZE:
½ cup confectioners' sugar

1½ tablespoons silver tequila

½ teaspoon lime zest (from about 1/2 lime)

¼ teaspoon salt

TO MAKE THE CAKE:

1. Preheat your air fryer to its appropriate cake setting, or 350°F.

2. Grease two 5 x 3 x 2-inch loaf pans with cooking spray.

3. In a food processor, blend the sugar and grapefruit zest.

4. In a medium bowl, whisk the flour, salt, and baking powder to combine.

5. In the bowl of a stand mixer fitted with the paddle attachment, mix the egg, sugar mixture, grapefruit juice, and vanilla extract on medium speed.

6. Set the mixer to low speed, and mix in the dry ingredients, being mindful to not overmix.

7. Fold in the vegetable oil and sour cream until they are fully incorporated.

8. Pour the batter into the prepared loaf pans and bake in

TO MAKE THE TEQUILA GLAZE:

1. In a small bowl, whisk the confectioners' sugar, tequila, lime zest, and salt together to combine. Drizzle the glaze over the cake right before serving.

the air fryer one at a time for 14 minutes each, or until a toothpick inserted into the center of the cake comes out mostly free of crumbs.

9. Let the cakes cool completely on a cooling rack before glazing.

Coconut Layer Cake with Vanilla Bean Buttercream

If you'd like to make this cake more tropical, feel free to swap out the vanilla buttercream for passion fruit, or even mango buttercream would work in this.

YIELD: one 2-layer, 6-inch cake   **PREP TIME:** 15 minutes
COOK TIME: 22 minutes

CAKE:

1 cup plus 2 tablespoons cake flour

1 teaspoon baking powder

¼ teaspoon salt

⅔ cup granulated sugar

6 tablespoons unsalted butter, at room temperature, cut into 1-inch pieces

3 large egg whites, at room temperature

½ cup coconut milk, at room temperature

¼ cup shredded unsweetened coconut

1 teaspoon vanilla extract

VANILLA BEAN BUTTERCREAM:

¾ cup (1½ sticks) unsalted butter, at room temperature

2 to 3 cups confectioners' sugar

½ vanilla bean, seeds scraped

¼ teaspoon vanilla extract

2 tablespoons whole milk

pinch of salt

TO MAKE THE CAKE:

1. Preheat your air fryer to its appropriate cake setting, or to 350°F.

2. Grease two 6-inch cake pans with cooking spray and line the bottoms with parchment paper.

3. In the bowl of a stand mixer fitted with the whisk attachment, whisk the cake flour, baking powder, and salt to combine.

4. With the speed set to low, mix in the sugar. Add the butter pieces and continue mixing for 1 minute more.

5. In a separate medium bowl, whisk together the egg whites, coconut milk, and shredded coconut. Pour the vanilla extract into the bowl and whisk to combine thoroughly.

6. Pour about half of the liquid mixture into the bowl of the stand mixer. Whisk on medium speed for 1 minute, making sure to scrape down the sides of the bowl. Add the remaining liquid mixture and mix well.

TO MAKE THE BUTTERCREAM:

1. In the bowl of stand mixer fitted with the paddle attachment, beat the butter on medium speed until creamy, about 2 minutes.

2. Mix the confectioners' sugar, vanilla bean seeds, vanilla extract, milk, and salt until you've reached your desired buttercream consistency.

7. Divide the batter between the two prepared cake pans, and bake in the air fryer one at a time for 11 minutes each, or until a toothpick inserted into the center of the cake comes out mostly free of crumbs.

8. Let the cakes cool completely on a cooling rack before frosting.

3. To frost the cake, slice the domes off each cake layer. Spread about one-third of the buttercream on top of the first layer. Repeat with the remaining layer, making sure to spread the buttercream on the sides of the cake as well.

Cookies and Cream Cake

Here we have a recipe that uses the "two step" or "two stage" method of cake baking. This involves mixing the dry ingredients (flour, sugar, baking soda, etc.) into the butter before the rest of the wet ingredients (eggs, extracts, etc.). Preparing your cake this way helps with the development of less gluten and also creates a more tender cake crumb. Try it!

YIELD: one 2-layer, 6-inch cake **PREP TIME:** 20 minutes
COOK TIME: 22 minutes

CAKE:
1 cup all-purpose flour

½ cup granulated sugar

⅛ teaspoon baking soda

¼ teaspoon baking powder

¼ teaspoon salt

6½ tablespoons unsalted butter, at room temperature

2 large egg whites, at room temperature

½ teaspoon vanilla extract

¼ cup full-fat sour cream, at room temperature

¼ cup whole milk, at room temperature

½ cup crushed cream-filled chocolate sandwich cookies

BUTTERCREAM:
¾ cup (1½ sticks) unsalted butter, at room temperature

2½ cups confectioners' sugar

1 teaspoon vanilla extract

2 tablespoons heavy cream

⅔ cup crushed cream-filled chocolate sandwich cookies

TO MAKE THE CAKE:

1. Preheat your air fryer to its appropriate cake setting, or 350°F.

2. Grease two 6-inch cake pans with cooking spray and line the bottoms with parchment paper.

3. In a small bowl, whisk together the flour, sugar, baking soda, baking powder, and salt to combine.

4. In the bowl of a stand mixer fitted with the paddle attachment, mix the butter on medium speed until creamy, about 2 minutes.

5. Mix the dry ingredients into the butter to fully incorporate, making sure to scrape the bowl as needed.

6. In a medium bowl, thoroughly whisk the egg whites, vanilla extract, sour cream, and milk, then pour the mixture into the butter mixture. Mix just to combine.

7. Fold the crushed cream-filled sandwich cookies into the cake batter. Divide the batter between the two prepared cake pans and bake in your air fryer one at a time for 11 minutes each, or until a toothpick inserted into the center of the cake comes out mostly free of crumbs.

8. Let the cakes cool completely before frosting.

TO MAKE THE BUTTERCREAM:

1. In the bowl of a stand mixer fitted with the paddle attachment, beat the butter on medium speed until creamy, about 2 minutes.

2. Mix in the confectioners' sugar, vanilla extract, and heavy cream until you've reached your desired buttercream consistency.

3. Fold in the crushed cream-filled sandwich cookies.

4. To frost the cake, slice the domes off each layer. Spread about one-third of the buttercream on top of bottom layer. Repeat with the top layer, and frost both the top and the sides of the cake.

Peanut Butter Layer Cake

Calling all peanut butter lovers: This cake is for you. There's peanut butter on every inch of this cake because life is short and peanut butter is delicious, as you already know.

YIELD: one 2-layer, 6-inch round cake
COOK TIME: 25 minutes
PREP TIME: 20 minutes

CAKE:

1¼ cups all-purpose flour

1½ teaspoons baking powder

¼ teaspoon salt

¼ cup (½ stick) unsalted butter, at room temperature

6 tablespoons granulated sugar

6 tablespoons packed light brown sugar

6 tablespoons creamy peanut butter

¼ cup full-fat sour cream, at room temperature

1 teaspoon vanilla extract

1 large egg, at room temperature

¼ cup whole milk, at room temperature

BUTTERCREAM:

½ cup (1 stick) unsalted butter, at room temperature

⅓ cup creamy peanut butter

2¼ cups confectioners' sugar

1½ tablespoons heavy cream or whole milk, at room temperature

TO MAKE THE CAKE:

1. Preheat your air fryer to its appropriate cake setting, or 350°F.

2. Grease two 6-inch cake pans and line the bottoms with parchment paper.

3. In a medium bowl, whisk the flour, baking powder, and salt to combine.

4. In the bowl of stand mixer fitted with the paddle attachment, cream the butter, granulated sugar, brown sugar, and peanut butter on medium speed until very light and fluffy, a good 3 to 4 minutes.

5. Add the sour cream and vanilla extract and mix very well. Add the egg and continue mixing, scraping the sides of the bowl as necessary.

6. Add the dry ingredients into the bowl of the stand mixer and the room temperature milk in alternating batches, being sure to begin and end with the dry ingredients, and mix until combined. Be mindful not to overmix the batter.

TO MAKE THE BUTTERCREAM:

1. In a large bowl using an electric hand-held mixer, cream the butter and peanut butter until smooth. Add the confectioners' sugar ¼ cup at a time and mix well. Pour in the heavy cream or milk and continue mixing until you've reached your desired buttercream consistency.

7. Divide the batter evenly between the prepared cake pans and bake in the air fryer one at a time for 12 minutes each, or until the cake is golden brown and a toothpick comes out mostly clean.

8. Let cool on a cooling rack while the buttercream is prepared.

2. To frost the cake, slice the domes off each layer. Spread about one-third of the buttercream on the first layer. Repeat with the remaining layer and buttercream, making sure to frost the sides of the cake.

Cappuccino Cake

This cake has a simple vanilla buttercream, but hazelnut or chocolate mocha frosting would work really well too.

YIELD: one 2-layer, 6-inch round cake   **PREP TIME:** 25 minutes
COOK TIME: 28 minutes

CAKE:

1½ cups all-purpose flour

1¼ teaspoons baking powder

¼ teaspoon salt

½ heaping teaspoon instant espresso powder

½ cup (1 stick) unsalted butter, at room temperature

¾ cups granulated sugar

2 tablespoons plus 2 teaspoons packed light brown sugar

2 large eggs, at room temperature

1 teaspoon vanilla extract

6 tablespoons whole milk, at room temperature

6 tablespoons fresh-brewed hot coffee

BUTTERCREAM:

½ cup (1 stick) unsalted butter, at room temperature

2¼ cups confectioners' sugar

1½ tablespoons heavy cream or whole milk, at room temperature

1 teaspoon vanilla extract

TO MAKE THE CAKE:

1. Preheat your air fryer to its appropriate cake setting, or 350°F.

2. Grease two 6-inch cake pans with cooking spray and line the bottoms with parchment paper.

3. In a medium bowl, whisk the flour, baking powder, salt, and espresso powder to combine.

4. In the bowl of a stand mixer fitted with the paddle attachment, cream the butter on medium speed until light and fluffy, 1 to 2 minutes. Add the granulated sugar and brown sugar, and continue mixing to combine. Crack in both eggs and mix to incorporate, scraping down the sides of the bowl as needed.

5. In alternating batches, add the dry ingredients and the milk to the bowl of the stand mixer on low speed, being mindful to begin and end with the dry ingredients. Mix just until combined.

6. With the mixer on low speed, pour in the fresh-brewed hot coffee and mix the batter until smooth.

TO MAKE THE BUTTERCREAM:

1. In a large bowl, cream the butter until smooth, 1 to 2 minutes. Add the confectioners' sugar ¼ cup at a time and mix well. Drizzle in the heavy cream or milk and vanilla extract, and mix until you've reached your desired buttercream consistency.

7. Divide the batter between the prepared cake pans and bake in the air fryer one at a time for 14 minutes each, or until a toothpick inserted into the cake comes out mostly free of crumbs.

8. Let the cakes cool on a cooling rack while the buttercream is prepared.

2. To frost the cake, slice the domes off each layer. Spread about one-third of the buttercream on the first layer. Repeat with the remaining layer and frost the top and sides of the cake.

Raspberry Mascarpone Cake

This simple vanilla cake is transformed into something special with tangy pureed raspberries and luscious mascarpone cheese. Be mindful not to overmix the frosting after the mascarpone has been added—doing so will result in the cheese breaking down and you'll end up with a thin, loose frosting. I also advise the use of a cake turntable or lazy Susan for decorating; it will make your life easier and you'll get to the "eat the cake" part much faster!

YIELD: one 2-layer, 6-inch round cake   **PREP TIME:** 25 minutes
COOK TIME: 28 minutes

CAKE:
1¼ cups all-purpose flour

1 cup granulated sugar

1½ teaspoons baking powder

½ teaspoon salt

½ cup whole milk, at room temperature

¼ cup vegetable oil

½ tablespoon vanilla extract

1 large egg, at room temperature

½ cup water, at room temperature

RASPBERRY FILLING:
½ cup fresh raspberries

1 tablespoon water

¼ cup sugar

1 tablespoon cornstarch

*1 teaspoon lemon zest
(from about 1 small lemon)*

BUTTERCREAM:
½ cup (1 stick) unsalted butter, at room temperature

2¼ cups confectioners' sugar

1½ tablespoons heavy cream or whole milk, at room temperature

1 teaspoon vanilla extract

4 ounces mascarpone cheese, at room temperature

TO MAKE THE CAKE:

1. Preheat your air fryer to its appropriate cake setting, or 350°F.

2. Grease two 6-inch cake pans with cooking spray and line the bottoms with parchment paper.

3. In a large bowl, whisk the flour, sugar, baking powder, and salt to combine.

4. In a medium bowl, whisk the milk, vegetable oil, vanilla extract, and egg very well to combine. Pour the wet ingredients into the bowl with the dry ingredients and whisk well to incorporate. Slowly pour in the water and mix well.

5. Divide the batter between the prepared cake pans and bake in

TO MAKE THE FILLING:

1. Using a food processor, puree the raspberries and water.

2. In a medium saucepan over medium heat, cook the sugar, cornstarch, lemon zest, and the raspberry puree until mixture

TO MAKE THE BUTTERCREAM:

1. In the bowl of stand mixer fitted with the paddle attachment, cream the butter and confectioners' sugar on medium speed until fluffy, 1 to 2 minutes. Add the vanilla and heavy cream or milk, and continue mixing.

TO DECORATE THE CAKE:

1. Slice off the domes of the cakes and place one layer on a cake turntable.

2. Fill a large pastry bag with about half of the frosting and pipe a border around the edge of the first layer to ensure the raspberry filling stays in place.

the air fryer one at a time for 14 minutes each, or until a toothpick inserted into the center of the cake comes out mostly free of crumbs.

6. Let the cakes cool on a cooling rack while the raspberry filling and frosting are prepared.

thickens and has come to a boil, 6 to 7 minutes. Continue to let the mixture boil for 1 minute more, then remove from the heat and push through a strainer to remove the raspberry seeds. Refrigerate while the frosting is prepared.

2. Add the softened mascarpone cheese to the bowl and mix until very well combined and you've reached your desired frosting consistency. Be mindful not to overmix the frosting, as the mascarpone will begin to thin out and break down.

3. Scoop about half of the raspberry filling on top of this cake layer and spread out to the frosting border.

4. Repeat with the top cake layer, adding frosting to the sides of the cake to cover.

Banana Cream Cake

This cake reminds me of my grandma, whose favorite pie is banana cream. When the recipe indicates "½ box instant banana pudding," you may make the entire box of pudding and only use half for the filling of this cake. Or, you can make half of the box and save the rest for later.

YIELD: one 2-layer, 6-inch round cake   **PREP TIME:** 25 minutes
COOK TIME: 26 minutes

CAKE:

½ *(3.9-ounce) box instant banana pudding mix*

1 cup plus 2 tablespoons all-purpose flour

1 teaspoon baking powder

¼ teaspoon baking soda

½ teaspoon salt

6 tablespoons unsalted butter, at room temperature

¾ cup granulated sugar

1 large egg, room temperature

1 teaspoon at vanilla extract

½ cup whole milk, at room temperature

BUTTERCREAM:

½ cup (1 stick) unsalted butter, at room temperature

2¼ cups confectioners' sugar

1½ tablespoons heavy cream or whole milk, at room temperature

1 teaspoon almond extract

½ teaspoon vanilla extract

vanilla wafers, for decorating (optional)

fresh banana, for decorating (optional)

TO MAKE THE CAKE:

1. Preheat your air fryer to its appropriate cake setting, or 350°F.

2. Grease two 6-inch cake pans and line the bottoms with parchment paper.

3. Prepare the banana pudding according to the package instructions. Refrigerate until ready to use.

4. In a medium bowl, whisk together the flour, baking powder, baking soda, and salt to combine.

5. In the bowl of a stand mixer fitted with the paddle attachment, cream the butter and sugar on medium speed until light and fluffy, 1 to 2 minutes. Crack in the egg and mix well. Pour in the vanilla extract and continue mixing.

6. In alternate batches add the dry ingredients and the milk to the wet ingredients, being sure to begin and end with the dry ingredients and being mindful not to overmix the batter.

TO MAKE THE BUTTERCREAM:

1. In the bowl of a stand mixer fitted with the paddle attachment, cream the butter on medium speed until fluffy, 1 to 2 minutes. Add confectioners' sugar ¼ cup at a

7. Divide the batter between the prepared cake pans.

8. Bake cakes in the air fryer one at a time for 13 minutes each, or until golden brown and a toothpick inserted into the cake comes out mostly free of crumbs.

9. Let the cakes cool on a cooling rack while the buttercream is prepared.

time and mix well. Add in the milk, almond extract, and vanilla extract and mix until you've reached your desired buttercream consistency.

TO DECORATE THE CAKE:

1. Slice off the domes of the cakes and place first layer on a cake turntable.

2. Fill a large pastry bag with about half of the buttercream and pipe a border around the edge of the bottom layer. Spread the prepared banana pudding on top of cake and out to the buttercream border. Place the second layer on top, and frost the top and sides of the cake.

3. Decorate the cake with vanilla wafers and slices of fresh banana, if desired.

Mint Chocolate Cake

This is probably my favorite cake in this book. It reminds me of the Andes mint chocolate candies a popular Italian restaurant I went to as a teenager would hand out after meals. A good decorating idea would be to line the border of the top layer of the cake with those Andes candies.

YIELD: one 2-layer, 6-inch round cake **PREP TIME:** 20 minutes
COOK TIME: 28 minutes

CAKE:

1¼ cups all-purpose flour

1 cup granulated sugar

6 tablespoons unsweetened Dutch-process cocoa powder

1 teaspoon baking soda

½ teaspoon salt

1 large egg, at room temperature

½ cup whole milk, at room temperature

½ cup vegetable oil

¾ teaspoon vanilla extract

½ cup fresh-brewed hot coffee

BUTTERCREAM:

½ cup (1 stick) unsalted butter, at room temperature

2¼ cups confectioners' sugar

1½ tablespoons heavy cream or whole milk, at room temperature

1 teaspoon peppermint extract

½ teaspoon vanilla extract

1 to 2 drops green gel food coloring

TO MAKE THE CAKE:

1. Preheat your air fryer to its appropriate cake setting, or 350°F.

2. Grease two 6-inch cake pans with cooking spray and line the bottoms with parchment paper.

3. In a large bowl, whisk together the flour, sugar, cocoa powder, baking soda, and salt to combine.

4. To the dry ingredients, add the egg, milk, and vegetable oil and mix well. Add the vanilla and mix again. Pour the fresh-brewed hot coffee into the batter and mix to incorporate. The batter will be thin.

5. Divide the batter into the prepared cake pans and bake in the air fryer one at a time for 14

minutes each, or until golden brown and a toothpick inserted into the center of the cake comes out mostly free of crumbs.

TO MAKE THE BUTTERCREAM:

1. In the bowl of a stand mixer fitted with the paddle attachment, cream the butter on medium speed until fluffy, 1 to 2 minutes. Add the confectioners' sugar ¼ cup at a time and mix to combine.

2. Pour in the heavy cream or milk, peppermint extract, vanilla extract, and gel food coloring and mix until you've reached your desired buttercream consistency.

6. Let the cakes cool on a cooling rack while the buttercream is prepared.

3. To frost the cake, slice the domes off each layer. Spread about one-third of the buttercream on the first layer. Repeat with the remaining layer and frost the sides of the cake.

Lemon Layer Cake with Blackberry Buttercream

An extremely summery cake.

YIELD: one 2-layer 6-inch round cake **PREP TIME:** 20 minutes
COOK TIME: 24 minutes

CAKE:

1¼ cups all-purpose flour

1¼ teaspoons baking powder

½ teaspoon salt

½ teaspoon vanilla extract

¼ cup whole milk, at room temperature

½ cup (1 stick) unsalted butter, at room temperature

½ cup plus 6 tablespoons granulated sugar

½ tablespoon lemon zest (from about 1 small lemon)

2 large eggs, at room temperature

BUTTERCREAM:

½ cup fresh blackberries

4 ounces (½ block) full-fat cream cheese, at room temperature

2 tablespoons unsalted butter, at room temperature

1½ cups confectioners' sugar

½ teaspoon almond extract

⅛ teaspoon salt

TO MAKE THE CAKE:

1. Preheat your air fryer to its appropriate cake setting, or 350°F.

2. Grease two 6-inch cake pans with cooking spray and line the bottoms with parchment paper.

3. In a medium bowl, whisk together the flour, baking powder, and salt to combine. In a small bowl, whisk the vanilla extract into the milk.

4. In the bowl of a stand mixer fitted with the paddle attachment, cream the butter, granulated sugar, and lemon zest on medium speed until fluffy, 1 to 2 minutes. Add the eggs one at a time and mix well after each addition.

5. In alternating batches, add the dry ingredients and the vanilla-milk mixture to the bowl of the stand mixer on low speed, being sure to begin and end with the dry ingredients. Do not overmix.

6. Divide the batter between the prepared cake pans and bake one at a time in the air fryer for 12 minutes each, or until golden brown.

7. Let the cakes cool on a cooling rack as the buttercream is prepared.

TO MAKE THE BUTTERCREAM:

1. Using a food processor, puree the blackberries. Push the puree through a sieve to remove the seeds.

2. In the bowl of a stand mixer fitted with the paddle attachment, beat the cream cheese and butter on medium speed until smooth and creamy. Add the confectioners' sugar ½ cup at a time and mix well. Add the almond extract and salt, and mix until you've reached your desired buttercream consistency.

3. To frost the cake, slice the domes off each layer. Spread about one-third of the buttercream on the first layer. Repeat with the second layer and frost the sides of the cake.

Kahlúa Chocolate Cake

A truly decadent cake for chocolate lovers. Kahlúa reminds me of Thanksgiving and Christmas, when my grandpa would make Mudslides for the adults. By heating up the Kahlúa for the buttercream, we're allowing the espresso powder to fully dissolve, leaving behind no awkward textures in the frosting.

YIELD: one 2-layer, 6-inch round cake   **PREP TIME:** 15 minutes
COOK TIME: 30 minutes

CAKE:

1 cup all-purpose flour

1 cup granulated sugar

6 tablespoons unsweetened Dutch-process cocoa powder

1 teaspoon baking soda

½ teaspoon salt

1 large egg, at room temperature

6 tablespoons whole milk, at room temperature

½ cup vegetable oil

¼ cup Kahlúa

½ teaspoon vanilla extract

6 tablespoons fresh-brewed hot coffee

BUTTERCREAM:

2 tablespoons Kahlúa

1 tablespoon instant espresso powder

¾ cup (1½ sticks) unsalted butter, at room temperature

2½ to 3 cups confectioner's sugar

pinch of salt

TO MAKE THE CAKE:

1. Preheat your air fryer to its appropriate cake setting, or 350°F.

2. Grease two 6-inch cake pans with cooking spray and line the bottoms with parchment paper.

3. In a large bowl, whisk the flour, sugar, cocoa powder, baking soda, and salt to combine. Add the egg, milk, vegetable oil, Kahlúa, and vanilla extract to the dry ingredients and mix very well to combine. Pour in the hot coffee and mix well. The batter will be thin.

4. Divide the batter between the prepared cake pans and bake in the air fryer one at a time for 14 to 15 minutes each, or until a toothpick inserted into the middle of the cake comes out mostly free of crumbs.

5. Let the cakes cool on a cooling rack while the buttercream is prepared.

TO MAKE THE BUTTERCREAM:

1. In a microwave, warm the Kahlúa for 2 minutes on high. Sprinkle in the instant espresso powder and stir to dissolve.

2. In the bowl of a stand mixer fitted with the paddle attachment, cream the butter on medium speed until smooth. Add the confectioners' sugar 1 cup at a time and mix very well. Add the Kahlúa mixture and the salt to the bowl and mix until you've reached your desired buttercream consistency.

3. To frost the cake, slice the domes off each layer. Spread about one-third of the buttercream on the first layer. Repeat with the second layer and frost the sides of the cake.

Black Forest Cake

I recommend placing the bowl to your stand mixer as well as the whisk attachment into the refrigerator about an hour prior to making the frosting. The chilled bowl and whisk, along with the cold heavy cream, will help to stabilize the whipped cream.

YIELD: one 2-layer, 6-inch round cake **PREP TIME:** 15 minutes
COOK TIME: 30 minutes

CAKE:

1 cup all-purpose flour

1 cup granulated sugar

6 tablespoons unsweetened Dutch-process cocoa powder

1 teaspoon baking soda

½ teaspoon baking powder

½ teaspoon salt

¼ cup vegetable oil

½ cup buttermilk, at room temperature

1 large egg, at room temperature

1 teaspoon vanilla extract

½ cup fresh-brewed hot coffee

1 cup fresh cherries, pitted and halved

WHIPPED CREAM FROSTING:

1½ cups very cold heavy whipping cream

2½ tablespoons confectioners' sugar, sifted

TO MAKE THE CAKE:

1. Preheat your air fryer to its appropriate cake setting, or 350°F.

2. Grease two 6-inch cake pans and line the bottoms with parchment paper.

3. In the bowl of stand mixer fitted with the paddle attachment, add the flour, sugar, cocoa powder, baking soda, baking powder, and salt, and mix on low speed to combine.

4. In a medium bowl, whisk the vegetable oil, buttermilk, egg, and vanilla extract very well to combine. Pour the wet ingredients into the dry ingredients and mix on low speed, gradually increasing speed until all ingredients have been combined.

5. Slowly pour in the hot coffee and mix well.

6. Divide the batter between the prepared cake pans and bake one at a time in the air fryer for 14 to 15 minutes, until a toothpick inserted into the middle of the cake comes out mostly free of crumbs.

7. Let the cakes cool on a cooling rack while the buttercream is prepared.

TO MAKE THE FROSTING:

1. In the cold bowl of a stand mixer fitted with the cold whisk attachment, add the heavy whipping cream and confectioners' sugar and beat on high speed until stiff peaks form.

TO ASSEMBLE THE CAKE:

1. Slice off the domes on the cake layers and spread about one-third of the whipped frosting on top of the first layer. Top with the fresh, halved cherries and repeat with the top layer. Frost the sides of the cake and decorate with more cherries, if desired.

Milk and Cookies Layer Cake

If you love to dunk your chocolate chip cookies into a big glass of cold milk, this cake is for you. I'm not aware of anyone who doesn't enjoy doing just that, so this cake is for everyone. If you don't want to bake cookies for the filling, *Ina Garten voice* store-bought chocolate chip cookies are fine.

YIELD: one 2-layer, 6-inch round cake   **PREP TIME:** 20 minutes
COOK TIME: 30 minutes

CAKE:
1¼ cups all-purpose flour

1½ teaspoons baking powder

¼ teaspoon salt

6 tablespoons unsalted butter, at room temperature

6 tablespoons granulated sugar

6 tablespoons packed light brown sugar

1½ teaspoons vanilla extract

¼ cup full-fat sour cream, at room temperature

1 large egg, at room temperature

¼ cup whole milk, at room temperature

¼ cup mini semisweet chocolate chips

BUTTERCREAM:
½ cup (1 stick) unsalted butter, at room temperature

2¼ cups confectioners' sugar

1½ tablespoons heavy cream or whole milk, at room temperature

1 teaspoon vanilla extract

FILLING:
6 chocolate chip cookies, plus more for decorating

⅓ cup whole milk

TO MAKE THE CAKE:

1. Preheat your air fryer to its appropriate cake setting, or 350°F.

2. Grease two 6-inch cake pans and line the bottoms with parchment paper.

3. In a medium bowl, whisk together the flour, baking powder, and salt to combine.

4. In the bowl of a stand mixer fitted with the paddle attachment, cream the butter, granulated sugar, and brown sugar on medium speed until very light and fluffy, 3 to 4 minutes. Add the vanilla extract and sour cream and mix very well. Crack in the egg and continue to mix, scraping down the sides of the bowl as needed.

5. In alternating batches, add the dry ingredients and the milk to the bowl of the stand mixer and mix on low speed to incorporate, being sure to begin and end with the dry ingredients. Be mindful not to overmix the batter. Fold in the mini chocolate chips by hand.

TO MAKE THE BUTTERCREAM:

1. In a large bowl, cream the butter with a hand-held mixer until smooth, 1 to 2 minutes. Add the confectioners' sugar ¼ cup at a time and mix well. Drizzle in the

TO ASSEMBLE THE CAKE:

1. Slice off the domes from the tops of the cake layers. Fill a large pastry bag with about one-third of the buttercream and pipe a border around the edge of the first cake layer.

2. Pour the milk for the filling into a small bowl, and dunk the cookies into the milk.

6. Divide the batter between the prepared cake pans and bake in the air fryer one at a time for 12 minutes each, or until a toothpick inserted into the center comes out mostly free of crumbs.

7. Let the cakes cool on a cooling rack while the buttercream is prepared.

heavy cream or milk and vanilla extract, and mix until you've reached your desired buttercream consistency.

3. Crumble the cookies and place on top of the first cake layer. Spread a thin layer of buttercream on top of the cookies, and frost the rest of the cake. Garnish with additional cookies around the edge of the top layer of the cake, if desired.

Peppermint Chip Cake

Peppermint baking chips are mostly sold around Christmas time; however, I found some in the middle of a warm April at my local Target in Atlanta. I will make this cake again for Christmas though, as it is a holiday cake through and through.

YIELD: one 2-layer, 6-inch round cake   **PREP TIME:** 25 minutes
COOK TIME: 26 minutes

CAKE:

1¼ cups all-purpose flour

2 teaspoons baking powder

¼ teaspoon salt

6 tablespoons unsalted butter, at room temperature

¾ cup granulated sugar

6 tablespoons full-fat sour cream, at room temperature

½ teaspoon vanilla extract

½ tablespoon peppermint extract

3 large egg whites, at room temperature

6 tablespoons whole milk, at room temperature

2 tablespoons peppermint baking chips

BUTTERCREAM:

6 tablespoons unsalted butter, at room temperature

2½ to 3 cups confectioners' sugar

2 to 2½ tablespoons heavy cream or whole milk

½ teaspoon vanilla extract

½ tablespoon peppermint extract

1 to 2 drops red gel food coloring (optional)

handful peppermint candy pieces, broken up

TO MAKE THE CAKE:

1. Preheat your air fryer to its appropriate cake setting, or 350°F.

2. Grease two 6-inch cake pans with cooking spray and line the bottoms with parchment paper.

3. In a medium bowl, whisk together the flour, baking powder, and salt to combine.

4. In the bowl of a stand mixer fitted with the paddle attachment, cream the butter and sugar very well on medium speed until light and fluffy, 3 to 4 minutes. Add the sour cream, vanilla extract, and peppermint extract, and mix very well. Add the egg whites and continue mixing to combine. Scrape down the sides of the bowl as needed.

5. In alternating batches, add the dry ingredients and the milk to the batter on low speed, making sure to begin and end with the dry ingredients and being mindful not to overmix the batter. Fold in the peppermint baking chips by hand.

TO MAKE THE BUTTERCREAM:

1. In the bowl of a stand mixer fitted with the paddle attachment, cream the butter on medium speed until smooth, 1 to 2 minutes. Add the confectioners' sugar 1 cup at a time and mix well. Drizzle in the heavy cream or milk, vanilla extract, peppermint extract, and gel food coloring, if using, and mix until you've reached your desired buttercream consistency. Fold in the broken peppermint pieces.

6. Divide the batter between the prepared cake pans and bake in the air fryer one at a time for 12 to 13 minutes, or until golden brown and a toothpick inserted in the center of the cake comes out mostly free of crumbs.

7. Let the cakes cool on a cooling rack while the buttercream is prepared.

2. To frost the cake, slice the domes off each layer. Spread about one-third of the buttercream on the first layer. Repeat with the remaining layer and frost the sides of the cake.

Raspberry Almond Cake

Yes, there are *two* raspberry-flavored cakes in this chapter. This cake has two buttercreams—almond and raspberry. Spread the raspberry buttercream in between the cake layers, and the almond buttercream on the top and sides when frosting the cake.

YIELD: one 2-layer, 6-inch round cake **PREP TIME:** 20 minutes
COOK TIME: 24 minutes

CAKE:

1¼ cups all-purpose flour

2 teaspoons baking powder

¼ teaspoon salt

6 tablespoons unsalted butter, at room temperature

¾ cup granulated sugar

6 tablespoons full-fat sour cream, at room temperature

½ tablespoon almond extract

3 large egg whites, at room temperature

6 tablespoons whole milk, at room temperature

RASPBERRY BUTTERCREAM:

¼ cup fresh raspberries

4 tablespoons unsalted butter, at room temperature

1½ cups confectioners' sugar

¼ teaspoon vanilla extract

ALMOND BUTTERCREAM:

6 tablespoons unsalted butter, at room temperature

2½ to 3 cups confectioners' sugar

2 tablespoons heavy cream or whole milk

1 teaspoon almond extract

TO MAKE THE CAKE:

1. Preheat your air fryer to its appropriate cake setting, or 350°F.

2. Grease two 6-inch cake pans with cooking spray and line the bottoms with parchment paper.

3. In a medium bowl, whisk together the flour, baking powder, and salt to combine.

4. In the bowl of a stand mixer fitted with the paddle attachment, cream the butter and sugar on medium speed until very light and fluffy, 3 to 4 minutes. Add the sour cream and almond extract and mix to combine. Add the egg whites and continue to mix.

5. In alternating batches, add the dry ingredients and the milk to the bowl of the stand mixer on low speed, making sure to begin and end with the dry ingredients and being mindful not to overmix the batter.

6. Divide the batter between the prepared cake pans and bake in the air fryer one at a time for 12 minutes each, or until golden brown and a toothpick inserted into the center of the cake comes out mostly free of crumbs.

7. Let the cakes cool on a cooling rack while the buttercreams are prepared.

TO MAKE THE RASPBERRY BUTTERCREAM:

1. In a food processor, puree the raspberries. Push the puree through a sieve to remove the seeds and set puree aside.

2. In the bowl of stand mixer fitted with the paddle attachment, cream the butter on medium speed until light and fluffy, 1 to 2 minutes. Add the confectioners' sugar ½ cup at a time and continue to mix. Add the vanilla extract and mix well.

3. Add the raspberry puree and continue to mix until you've reached your desired buttercream consistency.

TO MAKE THE ALMOND BUTTERCREAM:

1. In the bowl of a stand mixer fitted with the paddle attachment, cream the butter on medium speed until smooth, 1 to 2 minutes. Add the confectioners' sugar 1 cup at a time and mix well. Drizzle in the heavy cream or milk and almond extract, and mix until you've reached your desired buttercream consistency.

TO ASSEMBLE AND FROST THE CAKE:

1. Slice the domes off each cake layer. Spread all of the raspberry buttercream on the bottom cake layer. Place the second cake layer on top and spread about half of the almond buttercream on top, then spread the remaining almond buttercream on the sides of the cake and serve.

Sangria Layer Cake

I adapted this recipe from Liv For Cake, a popular food blogger from Vancouver, British Columbia. This brilliant cake has a strong sangria flavor, so if you aren't all that fond of red wine, I'd skip this recipe. For the wine lovers who will be making this cake, you can either make your own sangria or of course get your hands on a good-tasting bottled sangria. Feel free to bump up the pink color of the cake batter with a drop or two of fuchsia gel food coloring. Add fresh fruit in between the cake layers to really drive home the sangria flavors.

YIELD: one 2-layer, 6-inch round cake   **PREP TIME:** 20 minutes
COOK TIME: 26 minutes

CAKE:
1 cup plus 2 tablespoons all-purpose flour

1 teaspoon baking powder

¼ teaspoon salt

6 tablespoons unsalted butter, at room temperature

¾ cup granulated sugar

zest from ½ orange

1 large egg, at room temperature

¾ teaspoon vanilla extract

½ cup sangria, at room temperature

BUTTERCREAM:
½ cup (1 stick) unsalted butter, at room temperature

2¼ cups confectioners' sugar

1½ tablespoons heavy cream or whole milk, at room temperature

1 teaspoon vanilla extract

TO MAKE THE CAKE:

1. Preheat your air fryer to its appropriate cake setting, or 350°F.

2. Grease two 6-inch cake pans with cooking spray and line the bottoms with parchment paper.

3. In a medium bowl, whisk the flour, baking powder, and salt to combine.

4. In the bowl of a stand mixer fitted with the paddle attachment, cream the butter, granulated sugar, and orange zest on medium speed until very light and fluffy, 3 to 4 minutes. Crack in the egg and continue mixing, scraping down the sides of the bowl as needed. Pour in the vanilla and mix well.

5. In alternating batches, add the dry ingredients and the sangria to the cake batter, beating well after each addition and making sure to begin and end with the dry ingredients.

6. Divide the batter between the prepared cake pans and bake in the air fryer one at a time for 12 to 13 minutes each, or until a toothpick inserted into the center of the cake comes out mostly free of crumbs.

7. Let the cakes cool on a cooling rack while the buttercream is prepared.

TO MAKE THE BUTTERCREAM:

1. In the bowl of a stand mixer fitted with the paddle attachment, cream the butter on medium speed until smooth, 1 to 2 minutes. Add the confectioners' sugar ¼ cup at a time and mix well. Drizzle in the heavy cream or milk and vanilla extract, and mix until you've reached your desired buttercream consistency.

2. To frost the cake, slice the domes off each cake layer. Spread about one-third of the buttercream onto the first layer. Repeat with the remaining layer and frost the sides of the cake.

Pumpkin Brown Butter Cream Cheese Layer Cake

In this book, we have used solidified brown butter in a cake before (Brown Butter Cake with Toasted Almonds, page 10), and it's the same process for this cake. After browning the butter, remove from the heat and pour into a heat-resistant container, then refrigerate until it has solidified.

YIELD: one 2-layer, 6-inch round cake **PREP TIME:** 2 hours, 25 minutes
COOK TIME: 26 minutes

CAKE:

1 cup all-purpose flour

¾ teaspoon baking powder

¼ teaspoon baking soda

¼ teaspoon salt

1 teaspoon ground cinnamon

¼ teaspoon ground nutmeg

¼ cup (½ stick) unsalted butter, at room temperature

½ cup granulated sugar

¼ cup packed light brown sugar

1 large egg, at room temperature

½ cup canned pumpkin puree

2 tablespoons vegetable oil

1 teaspoon vanilla extract

6 tablespoons whole milk, at room temperature

BUTTERCREAM:

5 tablespoons unsalted butter, browned, cooled, and solidified (page 10)

4 ounces (½ block) full-fat cream cheese, softened

½ teaspoon vanilla extract

¼ teaspoon ground cinnamon

1½ to 2 cups confectioners' sugar

1 tablespoon milk

¼ teaspoon salt

TO MAKE THE CAKE:

1. Preheat your air fryer to its appropriate cake setting, or 350°F.

2. Grease two 6-inch cake pans with cooking spray and line the bottoms with parchment paper.

3. In a medium bowl, whisk together the flour, baking powder, baking soda, salt, cinnamon, and nutmeg to combine.

4. In the bowl of a stand mixer fitted with the paddle attachment, cream the butter, granulated sugar, and brown sugar on medium speed until very light and fluffy, 3 to 4 minutes. Crack in the egg and mix well, scraping down the sides of the bowl as needed. Add the pumpkin puree, vegetable oil, and vanilla extract to the bowl and mix well.

5. In alternating batches, add the dry ingredients and the milk to the batter on low speed, making sure to begin and end with the dry ingredients and being mindful not to overmix.

TO MAKE THE BUTTERCREAM:

1. In the bowl of a stand mixer fitted with the paddle attachment, cream the browned, solidified butter and cream cheese on medium speed until very fluffy, 3 to 4 minutes. Add the vanilla and cinnamon and continue mixing.

2. Add the confectioners' sugar ½ cup at a time, then the milk and salt, and mix until you've reached your desired buttercream consistency.

6. Divide the batter between the prepared cake pans and bake in the air fryer one at a time for 12 to 13 minutes each, or until a toothpick inserted in to the center comes out mostly free of crumbs.

7. Let the cakes cool on a cooling rack while the buttercream is prepared.

3. To frost the cake, slice the domes off each layer. Spread about one-third of the buttercream on top of the first layer and repeat with the remaining layer, making sure to frost the sides of the cake.

Cinnamon Roll Layer Cake

The cinnamon-sugar glaze goes in between layers, and the cinnamon buttercream follows. Serve this with a hot cup of coffee, or like me, with a giant iced latte.

YIELD: one 2-layer, 6-inch round cake **PREP TIME:** 20 minutes
COOK TIME: 26 minutes

CAKE:
1¼ cups all-purpose flour

2 teaspoons baking powder

½ teaspoon ground cinnamon

¼ teaspoon salt

6 tablespoons unsalted butter, at room temperature

¾ cups granulated sugar

6 tablespoons full-fat sour cream, at room temperature

1 teaspoon vanilla extract

3 large egg whites, at room temperature

6 tablespoons whole milk, at room temperature

CINNAMON-SUGAR GLAZE:
2½ tablespoons confectioners' sugar

1 tablespoon packed light brown sugar

½ tablespoon ground cinnamon

1 tablespoon water

CINNAMON BUTTERCREAM:
½ cup (1 stick) unsalted butter, at room temperature

½ teaspoon vanilla extract

½ teaspoon ground cinnamon

2½ cups confectioners' sugar

2 tablespoons heavy cream or whole milk

TO MAKE THE CAKE:

1. Preheat your air fryer to its appropriate cake setting, or 350°F.

2. Grease two 6-inch cake pans with cooking spray and line the bottoms with parchment paper.

3. In a medium bowl, whisk together the flour, baking powder, cinnamon, and salt to combine.

4. In the bowl of a stand mixer fitted with the paddle attachment, cream the butter and sugar on medium speed until very light and fluffy, 3 to 4 minutes. Add the sour cream and vanilla extract and continue to mix, scraping down the sides of the bowl as needed. Add the egg whites and mix to combine.

5. In alternating batches, add the dry ingredients and the milk to the bowl of the stand mixer on low speed, making sure to begin and end with the dry ingredients and being mindful not to overmix the batter.

6. Divide the batter between the prepared cake pans and bake in the air fryer one at a time for 13 minutes each, or until a toothpick inserted into the center of the cake comes out mostly free of crumbs.

7. Let the cakes cool on a cooling rack while the sugar glaze and buttercream are prepared.

TO MAKE THE CINNAMON-SUGAR GLAZE:

1. In a small bowl, whisk all ingredients until smooth and fully incorporated.

TO MAKE THE BUTTERCREAM:

1. In the bowl of a stand mixer fitted with the paddle attachment, cream the butter on medium speed until very fluffy, 3 to 4 minutes. Add the vanilla and cinnamon and continue mixing. Add the confectioners' sugar ½ cup at a time, and then the heavy cream or milk, and mix until you've reached your desired buttercream consistency.

TO FROST THE CAKE:

1. Slice the domes off each cake layer. Pour half of the cinnamon-sugar glaze on the bottom layer and spread to the edges. Drop about one-third of the cinnamon buttercream on top of the glaze/ bottom layer and spread to the edges. Repeat with the remaining cake layer, making sure to frost the sides of the cake with the cinnamon buttercream.

Peach Vanilla Cake

I live in Atlanta, where the peach situation is heavenly. This cake uses the freshest, most beautiful peaches you can imagine, but if they don't grow in abundance where you are, frozen will do.

YIELD: one 2-layer, 6-inch round cake **PREP TIME:** 35 minutes
COOK TIME: 26 minutes

CAKE:
1 cup plus 2 tablespoons cake flour

¾ teaspoon baking powder

pinch of salt

4½ tablespoons unsalted butter, at room temperature

½ cups granulated sugar

1 large egg, at room temperature

3½ tablespoons full-fat sour cream, at room temperature

1 teaspoon vanilla extract

¼ cup whole milk, at room temperature

FROSTING:
2½ cups sliced fresh peaches

2 tablespoons packed light brown sugar

¼ teaspoon ground cinnamon

¼ teaspoon salt

5 tablespoons unsalted butter, at room temperature

4 ounces (½ block) cream cheese, softened

2½ to 3 cups confectioners' sugar

½ teaspoon vanilla extract

1 tablespoon whole milk

TO MAKE THE CAKE:

1. Preheat your air fryer to its appropriate cake setting, or 350°F.

2. Grease two 6-inch cake pans with cooking spray and line the bottoms with parchment paper.

3. In a medium bowl, whisk together the flour, baking powder, and salt to combine.

4. In the bowl of a stand mixer fitted with the paddle attachment, cream the butter and sugar on medium speed until very light and fluffy, 3 to 4 minutes. Add the egg and continue to mix, scraping down the sides of the bowl as needed. Add the sour cream and vanilla extract and mix very well.

5. In alternating batches, add the dry ingredients and the milk to the bowl of the stand mixer on low speed, making sure to begin and end with the dry ingredients and being mindful not to overmix the batter.

6. Divide the batter between the prepared cake pans and bake in the air fryer one at a time for 13 minutes each, or until a toothpick inserted into the center of the cake comes out mostly free of crumbs.

7. Let the cakes cool on a cooling rack while the frosting is prepared.

TO MAKE THE FROSTING:

1. In a small bowl, add the peach slices, brown sugar, cinnamon, and salt. Stir the mixture and let sit on your counter for 10 minutes.

2. Using a food processor, puree the peach mixture until smooth. Pour the puree through a sieve and set aside.

3. In the bowl of a stand mixer fitted with the paddle attachment, cream the butter and cream cheese on medium speed until very

smooth, 3 to 4 minutes. Add the confectioners' sugar ½ cup at a time and mix well. Add the vanilla extract and the milk and continue to mix. Add the peach puree and mix very well until you've reached your desired consistency.

4. To frost the cake, slice the domes off each cake layer. Spread about one-third of the buttercream on the first layer. Repeat with the remaining layer, making sure to frost the sides of the cake.

Classic Vanilla Cake

The last two cakes in this chapter have classic flavors. This is a vanilla cake for those who like to keep things simple.

YIELD: one 2-layer, 6-inch round cake   **PREP TIME:** 15 minutes
COOK TIME: 24 minutes

CAKE:

1¼ cups all-purpose flour

¼ teaspoon baking powder

¼ teaspoon baking soda

½ teaspoon salt

½ cup (1 stick) unsalted butter, at room temperature

¾ cup granulated sugar

1 large egg, at room temperature

1 large egg yolk, at room temperature

1 teaspoon vanilla extract

½ cup buttermilk, at room temperature

BUTTERCREAM:

½ cup (1 stick) unsalted butter, at room temperature

2¼ cups confectioners' sugar

1½ tablespoons heavy cream or whole milk, at room temperature

1 teaspoon vanilla extract

TO MAKE THE CAKE:

1. Preheat your air fryer to its appropriate cake setting, or 350°F.

2. Grease two 6-inch cake pans with cooking spray and line the bottoms with parchment paper.

3. In a medium bowl, whisk the flour, baking powder, baking soda, and salt to combine.

4. In the bowl of stand mixer fitted with the paddle attachment, cream the butter and sugar on medium speed until very light and fluffy, 3 to 4 minutes. Crack in the egg and mix well. Add the egg

yolk and continue to mix, scraping down the sides of the bowl as needed. Add the vanilla; mix very well.

5. In alternating batches, add the dry ingredients and the buttermilk to the batter on low speed, making sure to begin and end with the dry ingredients and being mindful not to overmix.

6. Divide the batter between the prepared cake pans and bake in the air fryer one at a time for 11 to 12 minutes each, or until golden brown and a toothpick inserted into the center of the cake comes out mostly free of crumbs.

TO MAKE THE BUTTERCREAM:

1. In the bowl of a stand mixer fitted with the paddle attachment, cream the butter on medium speed until light and fluffy, 1 to 2 minutes. Add the confectioners' sugar ¼ cup at a time and mix well. Add the heavy cream or milk and the vanilla extract, and continue to mix until you've reached your desired buttercream consistency.

7. Let the cakes cool on a cooling rack while the buttercream is prepared.

2. To frost the cake, slice the domes off each cake layer. Spread about one-third of the buttercream on the bottom layer. Repeat with the top layer, making sure to frost the sides of the cake.

Dark Chocolate Cake with Ganache

I sometimes prefer a chocolate cake to have a ganache instead of being frosted with buttercream. I find a ganache helps to moisten the cake further, making this truly decadent and delicious.

YIELD: one 2-layer, 6-inch round cake **PREP TIME:** 20 minutes
COOK TIME: 28 minutes

CAKE:

1 cup all-purpose flour

¼ cup unsweetened Dutch-process cocoa powder

¼ teaspoon baking powder

¼ teaspoon baking soda

¼ teaspoon salt

½ cup (1 stick) unsalted butter, at room temperature

¾ cup packed light brown sugar

1 large egg, at room temperature

1 large egg yolk, at room temperature

3 ounces semisweet chocolate, melted

½ teaspoon vanilla extract

½ cup buttermilk, at room temperature

GANACHE:

1 cup heavy cream

¼ cup confectioners' sugar

⅛ teaspoon salt

8 ounces dark chocolate, roughly chopped

TO MAKE THE CAKE:

1. Preheat your air fryer to its appropriate cake setting, or 350°F.

2. Grease two 6-inch cake pans with cooking spray and line the bottoms with parchment paper.

3. In a medium bowl, whisk together the flour, cocoa powder, baking powder, baking soda, and salt to combine.

4. In the bowl of a stand mixer fitted with the paddle attachment, cream the butter and brown sugar on medium speed until very light and fluffy, 3 to 4 minutes. Add the egg and mix well. Add the egg yolk and continue to mix, scraping down the sides of the bowl as needed. Pour in the melted chocolate and vanilla extract and mix very well.

5. In alternating batches, add the dry ingredients and the buttermilk to the batter on low speed, making sure to begin and end with the dry ingredients and being mindful not to overmix the batter.

6. Divide the batter between the prepared cake pans and bake in the air fryer one at a time for 14 minutes each, or until a toothpick inserted into the center of the cake comes out mostly free of crumbs.

7. Let the cakes cool on a cooling rack while the ganache is prepared.

TO MAKE THE GANACHE:

1. In a large saucepan over medium heat, bring the heavy cream, confectioners' sugar, and salt to a boil.

2. Remove from the heat and pour over the roughly chopped chocolate in a heat-proof bowl. Let stand for 1 minute without stirring. Whisk just until combined.

3. Refrigerate until spreadable, about 1 hour.

TO GLAZE THE CAKE:

1. Place the bottom layer of the cake on a cooking rack that has been set over a baking sheet. Pour about half of the glaze over the first layer. Repeat with the top layer, letting the glaze drizzle over onto the sides of the cake.

Almond Cake with Mascarpone Cream Cheese Frosting and Cherry Drizzle

This recipe was inspired by my deep and unwavering love of a classic flavor combination: cherry and almond. Mascarpone is basically an acidic Italian cream cheese most commonly used in tiramisu. If the slight tanginess of mascarpone doesn't suit your taste buds, or if it's just too expensive at your grocery store that day, feel free to omit and bump up the cream cheese measurement to 4 ounces (or half of an 8-ounce block). If you are using sweet cherries for the drizzle, you may need to knock back the sugar measurement to 2 tablespoons. Similarly, if using sour cherries, adding an additional tablespoon of sugar to the ¼ cup will help to achieve balance. I adapted this cherry drizzle from popular food blog Smitten Kitchen.

YIELD: one 2-layer, 6-inch round cake   **PREP TIME:** 15 minutes
COOK TIME: 22 minutes

CHERRY DRIZZLE:
5 ounces sweet or sour cherries, pitted

1 tablespoon freshly squeezed lemon juice

¼ cup granulated sugar

½ tablespoon cornstarch

¼ cup water

CAKE:
1 cup all-purpose flour

1½ teaspoons baking powder

¼ teaspoon salt

6 tablespoons unsalted butter, at room temperature

½ cup plus 3 tablespoons granulated sugar

1½ teaspoon almond extract

1 large egg white, at room temperature

½ cup plus 1½ tablespoons almond milk

simple syrup, for brushing (optional)

MASCARPONE CREAM CHEESE FROSTING:
¼ cup mascarpone cheese

3 ounces full-fat cream cheese, softened

¼ cup (½ stick) unsalted butter, at room temperature

1 teaspoon vanilla extract

1½ cup confectioners' sugar

TO MAKE THE CHERRY DRIZZLE:

1. Bring all ingredients to a boil in a medium saucepan over medium heat. Once boiling, cook for an additional 1 to 2 minutes, until the mixture has thickened slightly. Remove from the heat and cool completely.

TO MAKE THE CAKE:

1. Preheat your air fryer to its appropriate cake setting, or 350°F.

2. Grease two 6-inch cake pans with cooking spray and line the bottoms with parchment paper.

3. In a medium bowl, whisk together the flour, baking powder, and salt.

4. In the bowl of a stand mixer fitted with the paddle attachment, cream the butter and sugar together on medium speed for 1 to 2 minutes until light and fluffy.

5. Mix in the almond extract, then mix in the egg white.

6. Add in the dry ingredients to the bowl of the stand mixer alternately with the almond milk, mixing well after each addition and being mindful to begin and end with the dry ingredients.

7. Divide the batter between the two prepared cake pans and bake one at a time in the air fryer for 11 minutes each, or until a toothpick inserted into the cake comes out mostly free of crumbs.

8. Let cool completely before frosting.

TO MAKE THE MASCARPONE CREAM CHEESE FROSTING:

1. In the bowl of a stand mixer fitted with the paddle attachment, cream together the mascarpone, cream cheese, and butter on medium speed for 1 to 2 minutes.

2. Mix the vanilla extract and confectioners' sugar until you've reached your desired frosting consistency.

TO ASSEMBLE THE CAKE:

1. Level off the domes of each cake layer and brush with simple syrup if desired.

2. Spread half of the frosting onto the first cake layer and smooth out with either a butter knife or offset spatula. You can also spoon some of the cherry drizzle on this layer, if you want to bump up the cherry flavor.

3. Place the second layer on top and spread the remaining frosting over the second layer and onto the sides. It's okay if some bits of cake are uncovered with frosting. This will just give you a trendy "naked" cake look, but feel free to double the frosting recipe here if you just prefer more of the stuff.

4. Spoon the remaining cherry drizzle over the top of the cake and serve.

PASTRIES

Settle in, I want to talk to you about air fryer pastry. The idea scared me a little, only because I wasn't sure what to expect. Would my tart dough shrink beyond recognition? Would pastry burn to a crisp? My concerns were put to rest when I took the first pastry out of the air fryer. It produced a pretty perfect-looking tart and as soon as I saw that, I felt confident. To get similar results, you'll need to use parchment paper, dried beans (I wouldn't use pie weights, only because I didn't test them in the air fryer, so I'm not sure how they would work out) for blind-baking, and mini tart pans.

My affection toward pastry has always been strong. Pastry is in another realm in the world of baking, one all its own. It is impressive, a challenge, and a great way to strengthen your baking skills. Pastry makes you feel like a real baker once you've mastered it. At least this is how it makes me feel. I hope these air fryer pastry recipes help you to either put your baking skills to good use or make pastry seem more approachable.

For the majority of these recipes, you'll really only be using the air fryer to blind-bake the pie or tart dough. From there, you'll build flavors using various pastry creams, stone fruit fillings, and chocolate ganache. Let's get pastry dough chilling, and let's get started.

Caramelized Apricot Tart with Cinnamon Pastry Cream

Two of my favorite flavors are used here: caramelized fruit and cinnamon. It's hard to be led astray when you're coming out the gate with such lovely flavors.

YIELD: four 4.75-inch tarts   **PREP TIME:** 5 hours, 15 minutes (includes chilling)
COOK TIME: 1 hour, 5 minutes

TART DOUGH:
1 large egg

1½ tablespoons granulated sugar

1 teaspoon salt

*2 cups all-purpose flour,
plus more for dusting*

*¾ cup (1½ sticks) cold unsalted
butter, cut into ¼-inch cubes*

CINNAMON PASTRY CREAM:
¾ cup heavy cream

2 tablespoons all-purpose flour

¼ cup granulated sugar

1 teaspoon ground cinnamon

pinch of salt

2 large egg yolks

½ teaspoon vanilla extract

CARAMELIZED APRICOTS:
4 apricots

2 tablespoons unsalted butter

6 tablespoons granulated sugar

*Fresh mint sprigs, for garnish
(optional)*

TO MAKE THE TART DOUGH:

1. Cut out four 8-inch parchment paper rounds using a standard-sized cake pan as a guide. Lightly grease each 4.75-inch tart pan with cooking spray.

2. In a small bowl, whisk the egg and set aside.

3. In a medium bowl, whisk together the sugar, salt, and flour to combine.

4. Add the cold butter to the flour mixture and toss with your fingers to coat the butter in the flour. Break up the butter either with your fingers or a pastry cutter until the majority of the butter is pea-sized, with some pieces slightly larger and some slightly smaller.

5. Pour in the egg to the flour mixture, and mix with your hands until the dough starts to come together. Turn the dough onto a floured surface and knead until smooth, a few minutes. Wrap the dough in plastic and refrigerate for 1 hour.

6. After an hour, let the dough rest on your counter for 5 minutes before rolling.

7. On a floured surface, give the dough a few whacks with your rolling pin, rotating the dough after each whack. Starting from the center, gently but firmly begin rolling the dough out to about ⅛ inch thick. Rotate the dough continuously to prevent it from sticking.

8. Using one of the tart pans as a mold, cut out four dough rounds slightly larger than the tart pans (by about 1 inch) with a knife.

TO MAKE THE PASTRY CREAM:

1. In a small saucepan over medium heat, warm the heavy cream until bubbles begin to form around the edges of the pan. Make sure to not boil the cream.

2. While the cream is warming, in a medium bowl, whisk together the flour, sugar, cinnamon, and salt. Add the egg yolks to this mixture, and whisk well.

3. Very slowly pour a little of the warm heavy cream into the flour-egg mixture to temper the eggs, whisking continuously.

Press and shape each dough round into each of the tart pans, being careful not to stretch the dough too much.

9. Pierce the bottoms of each tart with the tines of a fork, then preheat your air fryer to 350°F for 5 minutes. Place the prepared parchment rounds onto each tart round and fill with dried beans. Bake the tarts in the air fryer one at a time for 12 minutes each.

10. Remove the parchment paper and dried beans, rotate the tart 180 degrees to ensure even baking, and continue blind-baking for an additional 4 minutes per tart shell.

11. Let the tarts cool completely before adding pastry cream.

4. Pour the entire mixture back into the saucepan and set over medium heat, whisking constantly as it begins to thicken. Once large bubbles begin to surface, continue to whisk and let simmer for just a few more seconds.

5. Remove from the heat and stir in the vanilla extract. Pour the pastry cream into a bowl, and press plastic wrap onto the surface of the cream to prevent a skin from forming. Refrigerate for at least 3 hours.

TO MAKE THE CARAMELIZED APRICOTS:

1. Halve the apricots, and carefully remove the pits using a spoon. Then slice each into half-moons.

2. In a sauté pan set over medium heat, melt the butter. Add the sugar and stir to dissolve. Swirl the mixture occasionally for about 4 minutes, until light brown in color.

3. Add the sliced apricot pieces and caramelize until the sugar has turned a deep amber color, about 5 minutes.

4. Remove from the heat and immediately begin assembling the tarts.

TO ASSEMBLE THE TARTS:

1. Spoon about ¼ cup of the pastry cream into each tart.

2. Spoon the caramelized apricot slices onto the pastry cream and sprinkle with a fresh mint sprig, if desired. Serve immediately.

Mexican Chocolate Ganache Tarts

One of my favorite things to do in baking is use the flavors from the Mexican food I grew up cooking and eating. This recipe uses ancho chile powder, which has a great smokiness to it. Combined with the semisweet chocolate, the mild ancho heat makes these tarts something special.

YIELD: four 4.75-inch tarts **PREP TIME:** 1 hour, 20 minutes (includes chilling)
COOK TIME: 1 hour, 5 minutes

Tart Dough (page 85)

6 ounces semisweet chocolate, roughly chopped

¾ cup heavy cream

1 teaspoon vanilla extract

¼ teaspoon ground cinnamon

¼ teaspoon ancho chile powder

TO MAKE THE TARTS:

1. Prepare the tart dough as instructed. Fit the dough into four 4.75-inch tart pans and bake according to the recipe directions.

2. After the tarts have baked and cooled, place the chopped chocolate in a heatproof bowl.

3. In a small saucepan set over medium heat, warm the heavy cream until bubbles begin to form around the edges of the pan. Remove from the heat.

4. Pour the heavy cream over the chopped chocolate and let sit for 30 seconds.

5. Carefully whisk the chocolate and heavy cream just until combined and smooth. Pour in the vanilla extract, then add the ground cinnamon and ancho chile powder to the ganache. Whisk one last time to combine.

6. Distribute ganache evenly among the four tart shells and refrigerate for about 2 hours, or until the chocolate has set.

Peach Pecan Tarts
with Caramel Drizzle

I can't think of anything tastier than a dessert with sweet and salty components. Use fresh peaches if available, but frozen will do in a pinch or if they aren't in season.

YIELD: four 4.75-inch tarts **PREP TIME:** 1 hour, 15 minutes
COOK TIME: 44 minutes

¼ cup whole pecans

Tart Dough (page 85)

Caramel Drizzle (page 19)

½ cup diced peaches (from about 1 to 2 peaches), in ½-inch pieces

1 tablespoon granulated sugar

½ teaspoon ground cinnamon

½ teaspoon ground nutmeg

½ teaspoon vanilla extract

TO TOAST THE PECANS:

1. In a dry skillet over medium heat, toast the pecans until they give off a nutty aroma, 3 to 4 minutes. Be mindful to stir the pecans constantly to avoid burning. Transfer the pecans to a cutting board and give them a rough chop, then measure 2 tablespoons and set aside.

TO MAKE THE TARTS:

1. Prepare the tart dough as instructed. Fit the dough into four 4.75-inch tart pans and refrigerate while the caramel drizzle and peach filling are prepared.

2. Prepare the caramel drizzle as instructed. Set aside to cool.

3. Preheat your air fryer to 375°F for 10 minutes.

4. Toss the peach pieces in a medium bowl. Sprinkle in the sugar, cinnamon, nutmeg, vanilla extract, and toasted, chopped pecans.

5. Divide the peach filling evenly among the tart shells, and bake one at a time in the air fryer for 11 minutes each.

6. Drizzle each tart with the caramel right before serving.

Classic Apple Pie

I knew for sure I wanted to test an apple pie in the air fryer and I'm so glad I did. I'd never baked a 6-inch pie before, and it was a nice change from a traditional 8-inch pie. I used Gala apples here, but Granny Smith is also a solid option for baking.

YIELD: one 6-inch pie **PREP TIME:** 1 hour, 10 minutes (includes chilling)
COOK TIME: 30 minutes

PIE DOUGH:

1½ cups all-purpose flour

¼ teaspoon salt

¼ teaspoon granulated sugar

½ cup (1 stick) cold unsalted butter, cut into ¼-inch cubes

3 tablespoons ice-cold water

APPLE FILLING:

2 medium Gala apples, peeled and diced

2 teaspoons freshly squeezed lemon juice (from about 1 lemon)

zest from 1 lemon

½ teaspoon vanilla extract

1 tablespoon ground cinnamon

2½ tablespoons granulated sugar

1½ tablespoons unsalted butter

1 large egg, beaten

TO MAKE THE PIE DOUGH:

1. In a medium bowl, whisk the flour, salt, and sugar just to combine.

2. Toss in the cold butter cubes, and cut into the flour mixture either with your hands or a pastry cutter. The butter should be cut into mostly pea-sized pieces, with some pieces that are larger and some smaller.

3. Pour the water into the flour-butter mixture and toss lightly until the dough begins to hold together. Turn the dough onto a lightly floured surface and shape into two disks. Wrap each disk with plastic and refrigerate for about an hour.

TO MAKE THE FILLING:

1. Combine the apples, lemon juice, lemon zest, and vanilla extract in a medium bowl. In a small bowl, whisk the cinnamon and sugar to combine. Sprinkle the cinnamon/sugar mixture over the apples and toss to coat. Set aside while you roll out the dough.

TO ASSEMBLE THE PIE:

1. Once the dough is chilled, set it on your counter for about 5 minutes to come to room temperature.

2. On a lightly floured surface, roll one of the dough disks out to a 10-inch circle about ¼ inch thick, turning the dough as you go to help it form a circle.

3. Preheat your air fryer to 320°F for about 10 minutes. Lightly grease a 6-inch pie pan with cooking spray.

4. Fit the dough into the pie plate, being mindful to not stretch the dough too much. Spoon the apple filling into the pie pan and dot with butter. Set the pie plate into the refrigerator to chill while you roll out the second dough disk.

5. Repeat step 2 with the remaining dough, and gently place the dough on top of the apple filling.

6. Crimp the edges of the dough, then brush with the egg and set back into the refrigerator to chill for about 5 minutes.

7. Bake the apple pie in your air fryer for 25 to 30 minutes, or until the pastry is golden brown.

Plum Tart with Dark Chocolate Drizzle

These are very sophisticated flavors. The slight bitterness of dark chocolate works well with the sweet plums.

YIELD: one 6-inch tart   **PREP TIME:** 1 hour, 20 minutes (includes chilling)
COOK TIME: 20 minutes

PLUM TART:
2 tablespoons whole almonds

Tart Dough (page 85)

¼ cup granulated sugar, divided

¼ teaspoon ground cinnamon

1 tablespoon all-purpose flour, plus more for dusting

3 to 4 plums, halved, pitted, and sliced into half-moons

1 large egg, beaten, for brushing

DARK CHOCOLATE DRIZZLE:
2 ounces dark chocolate, roughly chopped and melted

TO MAKE THE TART:

1. In a dry skillet over medium heat, toast the almonds until they give off a nutty aroma and have lightly browned, 3 to 4 minutes. Set aside to cool.

2. Prepare the tart dough as instructed. Roll out the dough on a lightly floured surface to about 8-inches in diameter. Gently fit the tart dough into a 6-inch tart pan and refrigerate while the plum filling is prepared.

3. Preheat your air fryer to 350°F for 10 minutes.

4. Using a food processor, pulse the toasted almonds, 3 tablespoons of the sugar, cinnamon, and flour until coarsely ground. Sprinkle the almond-flour mixture over the bottom of the tart.

5. Arrange plum half-moons on top of the dough, spacing them close together. Brush the edges of the tart with the beaten egg.

6. Bake the tart in your air fryer for 20 minutes, or until the pastry is golden brown and the plum filling is bubbling slightly.

TO MAKE THE DARK CHOCOLATE DRIZZLE:

1. Over a double boiler, melt the dark chocolate. Stir constantly with a rubber spatula until the chocolate is melted and completely smooth. Once the tart has cooled, drizzle the melted dark chocolate over the top and serve.

Chocolate Silk Pie

In my lifetime I have eaten a ton of chocolate silk pie, all store-bought and from the frozen section though. Making my own felt like giving myself a gift, which of course is exactly what a pie is.

YIELD: one 6-inch pie **PREP TIME:** 6 hours, 10 minutes (includes chilling)
COOK TIME: 18 minutes

Pie Dough (page 90)

⅓ cup granulated sugar

1 large egg

2 ounces semisweet chocolate, melted

½ teaspoon vanilla extract

2 tablespoons plus 2 teaspoons unsalted butter, softened

⅓ cup heavy whipping cream

1 teaspoon confectioners' sugar

TO MAKE THE PIE:

1. Preheat your air fryer to 350°F for 10 minutes.

2. Roll out the dough to about 8-inches in diameter. Fit dough the into a 6-inch pie plate and crimp the edges. Set parchment paper over the dough and fill the inside with dried beans. Blind-bake the pie crust in the air fryer for 14 minutes.

3. Remove the parchment paper and dried beans. Turn the pie 180 degrees to ensure even browning and baking. Continue blind-baking the crust for an additional 4 to 5 minutes. Let the crust cool completely before filling.

4. In a small saucepan over low heat, whisk the sugar and egg to combine very well. Cook and stir constantly until mixture has reached 160°F on a digital thermometer, 5 to 7 minutes. Remove from the heat.

5. Stir in the chocolate and vanilla extract. Set aside to cool, being mindful to stir occasionally.

6. With an electric hand-held mixer, cream the butter in a medium bowl until light and fluffy, about 2 minutes. Pour in the cooled chocolate mixture and continue mixing until very well incorporated.

7. In the bowl of a stand mixer fitted with the whisk attachment and set to medium-high speed, whisk the heavy cream until soft peaks form, about 5 minutes. Increase the mixing speed to high, sprinkle in the confectioners' sugar, and continue mixing until stiff peaks form, another 2 minutes. Fold the whipped cream into the chocolate mixture.

8. Pour the chocolate filling into the blind-baked pie crust and refrigerate until set, at least 6 hours. Garnish with more whipped cream and chocolate shavings before serving, if desired.

Lemon Pastry Cream Tarts with Fresh Berries

These tarts are very cute and have flavors that are perfect for a cool spring day. Use a mixture of berries, or one variety of your favorite berry. I used raspberries and blackberries, my favorites.

YIELD: four 4.75-inch tarts **PREP TIME:** 3 hours, 10 minutes
COOK TIME: 1 hour, 5 minutes

Tart Dough (page 85)

¾ cup heavy cream

2 tablespoons all-purpose flour

¼ cup granulated sugar

pinch of salt

2 large egg yolks

½ teaspoon vanilla extract

2 heaping teaspoons lemon zest (from about 2 small lemons)

1½ to 2 cups fresh berries, rinsed and dried

confectioners' sugar, for sprinkling (optional)

TO MAKE THE TARTS:

1. Prepare the tart dough as instructed. Right before rolling out the dough, preheat your air fryer to 350°F for 10 minutes.

2. Roll out the dough and fit into four 4.75-inch tart pans. Pierce the bottoms of the tarts with the tines of a fork. Place a piece of parchment paper atop each of the tarts and fill with dried beans. Blind-bake one tart in the air fryer for 12 minutes.

3. Remove the parchment paper and dried beans, rotate the tart 180 degrees to ensure even baking, and continue blind-baking for 4 minutes. Repeat blind-baking process, one at a time, with the remaining tarts.

4. Let the tart shells cool completely while the pastry cream is prepared.

5. For the pastry cream, in a small saucepan set over medium heat, warm the heavy cream until bubbles begin to form around the edges of the pan. Make sure to not boil the cream.

6. While the cream is warming, in a medium bowl, whisk the flour, sugar, and salt to combine. Add the egg yolks to this mixture, and whisk well.

7. Very slowly pour a little of the warm heavy cream into the flour-egg mixture to temper the eggs, whisking continuously.

8. Pour the entire mixture back into the saucepan and set over medium heat, whisking constantly as it begins to thicken. Once large bubbles begin to surface, continue to whisk and let simmer for just a few more seconds.

TO ASSEMBLE THE TARTS:

1. Spoon about ¼ cup pastry cream into each tart shell. Arrange the berries atop the pastry cream,

9. Remove from heat and stir in the vanilla extract and lemon zest. Pour the pastry cream into a bowl and press plastic wrap onto the surface of the cream to prevent a skin from forming. Refrigerate for at least 3 hours.

sprinkle with confectioners' sugar, if desired, and serve.

Apple Custard Tarts

I wish I had made these tarts in the fall, but these apple custard tarts work year-round. Use your favorite baking apple. I did not peel the apples for this, as I tend to like the look of an unpeeled baked apple far more than a peeled one. Feel free to peel your apples if you want, though. If you really wanted to go heavy with fall flavors, try adding ½ teaspoon ground cinnamon to the tart dough.

YIELD: four 4.75-inch tarts   **PREP TIME:** 30 minutes   **COOK TIME:** 1 hour

CRUST:
¾ cups graham cracker crumbs (from about 5 graham cracker sheets)

3 tablespoons unsalted butter, melted

2 tablespoons plus 2 teaspoons granulated sugar

FILLING:
¾ cup whole milk

1 teaspoon vanilla extract

2 large egg yolks

3 tablespoons granulated sugar, plus 1 tablespoon more for sprinkling

2 tablespoons cornstarch

2 small Gala apples, cored and thinly sliced

TO MAKE THE CRUST:

1. In a small bowl, combine the graham cracker crumbs with the melted butter and granulated sugar. Using a rubber spatula, toss the crumbs and melted butter with the sugar to combine.

2. Press the graham cracker crust into the bottoms and up the sides of four 4.75-inch tart pans. Set aside while the filling is prepared.

TO MAKE THE FILLING:

1. Pour the milk and vanilla extract into a small saucepan and bring to a gentle boil.

2. While the milk gets hot, in a small bowl whisk the egg yolks, 3 tablespoons of the granulated sugar, and the cornstarch to combine.

3. Preheat your air fryer to 350°F for 10 minutes.

4. Once the milk has boiled, slowly whisk a little of it into the egg mixture. Pour everything back into the saucepan and bring the mixture back to a boil. Remove from the heat and set aside to cool slightly.

5. Pour the custard into the prepared graham cracker crusts and arrange the apple slices atop the custard.

6. Sprinkle the tops of each tart with the remaining granulated sugar, and bake the tarts in the air fryer one at a time for 14 to 15 minutes each, or until the pastry is golden brown and the custard has set. Let the tarts cool slightly before serving.

Caramel Apple Turnovers

These turnovers put caramel and apple in the front and center, where this classic flavor combination should always be.

YIELD: 8 turnovers   **PREP TIME:** 25 minutes   **COOK TIME:** 48 minutes

CARAMEL APPLE FILLING:
2 medium Granny Smith apples, peeled and diced

3 tablespoons unsalted butter

½ cup packed light brown sugar

1 teaspoon vanilla extract

1 teaspoon freshly squeezed lemon juice

zest from 1 lemon

½ teaspoon ground cinnamon

¼ teaspoon salt

PASTRY:
1 large egg

1 tablespoon water

2 sheets frozen puff pastry, thawed

TO MAKE THE FILLING:

1. In a medium saucepan over medium heat, combine all the filling ingredients. Simmer everything until the apples become slightly tender and a syrup has developed, about 10 minutes. Set aside to cool while the pastry is prepared.

TO PREPARE THE PASTRY:

1. In a small bowl, whisk the egg and water to make an egg wash.

2. Place one sheet of puff pastry onto a clean surface and divide into four equally sized squares. Spoon about 2 tablespoons of the filling onto the middle of each square.

3. Brush the edges of each square with the egg wash, then fold each diagonally to form a turnover. Seal the edges of each turnover with a fork and refrigerate while the remaining turnovers are prepared.

4. Preheat your air fryer to 350°F for 10 minutes, then repeat steps 2 and 3 with the remaining puff pastry.

5. Brush the tops of all 8 turnovers with the egg wash and cut a few slits into each.

6. Place 4 turnovers into the air fryer and bake until golden brown, about 19 minutes. Repeat with the remaining turnovers. Serve warm or at room temperature.

Raspberry Chocolate Tarts

One of my all-time favorite flavor combinations. The bright tartness of the raspberry combined with decadent chocolate ganache is classic for a reason.

YIELD: four 4.75-inch tarts **PREP TIME:** 50 minutes **COOK TIME:** 2 hours, 10 minutes (includes chilling)

Tart Dough (page 85)

¾ cup heavy cream

3 ounces milk chocolate, chopped

2 tablespoons chocolate hazelnut spread

1 teaspoon amaretto (optional)

fresh raspberries

TO MAKE THE TARTS:

1. Prepare the tart dough as instructed. Right before rolling out the dough, preheat your air fryer to 350°F for 10 minutes.

2. Roll out the dough and fit it into four 4.75-inch tart pans. Pierce the bottoms of the tarts with the tines of a fork. Place a piece of parchment paper atop each of the tarts and fill with dried beans. Blind-bake one tart in the air fryer for 12 minutes.

3. Remove the parchment paper and dried beans, rotate the tart 180 degrees to ensure even baking, and continue blind-baking for 4 minutes. Repeat blind-baking process one at a time with the remaining tarts.

4. Let the tart shells cool completely while the ganache is prepared.

5. For the ganache, once the tarts have baked and cooled, place the chopped milk chocolate in a heatproof bowl.

6. In a small saucepan over medium heat, warm the heavy cream until bubbles begin to form around the edges of the pan. Remove from the heat.

7. Pour heavy cream over the chopped chocolate and let sit for 30 seconds. Carefully whisk the chocolate and heavy cream just until combined and smooth. Spoon in the chocolate hazelnut spread and the amaretto, if using. Whisk one last time to combine.

8. Distribute the ganache evenly among the four tart shells and chill for about 2 hours, or until the chocolate has set. Once the ganache has set, top each tart with fresh raspberries and serve.

S'mores Tarts

Make these for your kids! Or make these whenever you want to feel like a kid yourself.

YIELD: four 4.75-inch-inch tarts **PREP TIME:** 30 minutes **COOK TIME:** 2 hours, 28 minutes (includes chilling)

CRUST:
¾ cups graham cracker crumbs (from about 5 graham cracker sheets)

3 tablespoons unsalted butter, melted

2 tablespoons plus 2 teaspoons granulated sugar

GANACHE:
6 ounces milk chocolate, chopped

½ cup heavy cream

2 tablespoons unsalted butter, cubed

MARSHMALLOW TOPPING:
1 large egg white, at room temperature

¼ cup granulated sugar

⅛ teaspoon cream of tartar

½ teaspoon vanilla extract

TO MAKE THE CRUST:

1. Preheat your air fryer to 350°F for 10 minutes.

2. In a small bowl, combine the graham cracker crumbs with the melted butter and granulated sugar. Using a rubber spatula, toss the crumbs and melted butter with the sugar to combine.

3. Press the graham cracker crust into the tart pans and bake the tarts in the air fryer one at a time for 7 minutes each. Let the tarts cool completely before filling.

TO MAKE THE GANACHE:

1. Once the tarts have baked and cooled, place the chopped milk chocolate in a heatproof bowl.

2. In a small saucepan over medium heat, warm the heavy cream until bubbles begin to form around the edges of the pan. Remove from the heat.

3. Pour the heavy cream over the chopped chocolate and let sit for 30 seconds.

4. Carefully whisk the chocolate and heavy cream just until combined and smooth. Stir in the butter and whisk one last time to combine.

5. Distribute the ganache evenly among the four tart shells and refrigerate for 2 hours, or until the chocolate has set.

TO MAKE THE MARSHMALLOW TOPPING:

1. Place the egg white, sugar, and cream of tartar in a heatproof bowl. Set the bowl over a saucepan filled with an inch or two of simmering water to create a double-boiler.

2. Whisk constantly until the sugar has dissolved, about 5 minutes. Transfer to the bowl of a stand mixer fitted with the whisk attachment.

3. On high speed, mix the egg white and sugar mixture for about 5 minutes or until soft, glossy peaks form. Add the vanilla extract and stir just to combine.

TO ASSEMBLE TARTS:

1. Remove tarts from the refrigerator and spoon a couple dollops of the marshmallow meringue on top of each one. If you have a kitchen torch, toast the marshmallow, of course. Serve immediately.

Peach Pie Turnovers

These are just like the Caramel Apple Turnovers (page 100), only this time in peach pie form. I highly recommend using fresh peaches for this.

YIELD: 8 turnovers   **PREP TIME:** 25 minutes   **COOK TIME:** 20 minutes

1 large egg

1 tablespoon water

2 cups diced peaches (from about 2 medium peaches)

2 teaspoons packed dark brown sugar

4 teaspoons granulated sugar, divided

½ teaspoon salt

½ teaspoon ground cinnamon

juice from 1 small lemon

2 sheets frozen puff pastry, thawed

TO MAKE THE TURNOVERS:

1. Preheat your air fryer to 350°F for 10 minutes.

2. In a small bowl, whisk the egg and tablespoon of water to make an egg wash. Set aside.

3. In a medium bowl, combine the diced peaches, brown sugar, 3 teaspoons of the granulated sugar, salt, cinnamon, and lemon juice. Let sit for 10 minutes.

4. Unfold the puff pastry sheets onto a lightly floured surface. Cut each pastry sheet into four equally sized rectangles.

5. Top one half of each pastry rectangle with peach filling. Fold the pastry over to form a triangle.

6. With a fork, press and seal the pastry edges together. Repeat with remaining rectangles.

7. Brush each turnover with the egg wash, sprinkle the tops of each with the leftover granulated sugar, and cut a few slits into the pastries.

8. Fit a piece of parchment paper onto the bottom of the air fryer basket. Place 4 turnovers into the basket and bake for 10 minutes, or until the turnovers are golden brown. Repeat with the remaining 4 turnovers. Serve warm.

Cherry Pie

Letting the chilled pie dough rest on your counter allows it to come to room temperature, making it easier to roll out. Cherry pie reminds me of *Twin Peaks*, which reminds me of the '90s and being a kid. I'm confident Dale Cooper would appreciate the air fryer version of his favorite pie.

YIELD: one 6-inch pie **PREP TIME:** 1 hour, 15 minutes (includes chilling)
COOK TIME: 25 minutes

Pie Dough (page 90)

½ cup granulated sugar

1½ tablespoons cornstarch

⅛ teaspoon salt

2 cups fresh cherries, stemmed and pitted

½ teaspoon vanilla extract

1 teaspoon freshly squeezed lemon juice

1 large egg, lightly beaten

1 tablespoon water

1 tablespoon cold unsalted butter, cut into small cubes

TO MAKE THE PIE:

1. Prepare the pie dough as instructed. Shape the dough into two small disks, one slightly larger than the other. Refrigerate the dough while the cherry filling is prepared.

2. To make the cherry filling, whisk the granulated sugar, cornstarch, and salt in a small bowl to combine.

3. Place the cherries in a medium bowl, sprinkle with the sugar mixture, and toss to coat. Add the vanilla and the freshly squeezed lemon juice, and toss to combine.

4. Remove the pie dough from the refrigerator and place on the counter for about 5 minutes to bring to room temperature.

5. Preheat your air fryer to 350°F for 10 minutes. Whisk the egg lightly with the water for an egg wash and set aside.

6. On a lightly floured surface, roll the larger dough disk into a circle with about an 8-inch diameter and ⅛-inch thickness. Fit the dough into the pie plate and trim the edges, leaving about a 1-inch overhang.

7. Spoon the cherry filling into the pie and dot the top with the cubed butter. Refrigerate while the second dough disk is rolled out.

8. Roll out the second dough disk on a lightly floured surface to fit the pie plate. Remove the pie from the refrigerator. Fit the second round of dough on top of the cherry filling, and crimp the edges.

9. Make 3 slits onto the top of the pie, brush the top and edges with the egg wash, and bake in your air fryer for 25 minutes, or until golden brown. Serve warm.

COOKIES

If you haven't noticed by now, small batch is your friend when baking with the air fryer. The same continues to be true with air fryer cookies. These air fryer versions are slightly crispier than standard oven-baked cookies, but they still make for a great dessert.

A note: Most of these recipes yield about 8 to 15 cookies, so if you'd like to double up, just keep in mind that you'll be baking in batches of four. This can be quite time-consuming, so I suggest using your oven in lieu of the air fryer if you're planning on making a standard two dozen or more cookies. Before I started baking in the air fryer, I don't think I appreciated small batch very much. I thought, "Why make just half a dozen cookies when a dozen means more cookies?" The beauty in small batch baking is plentiful though. If you are a family of one, if you are trying to reduce your dessert intake, or if you just don't want to deal with having a lot of leftover cookies, small batch is for you.

You will be baking these cookies in the air fryer basket. Very small cookie sheets really don't exist (yet?), so I initially didn't even think air fryer cookies could be done. Turns out you can just use the air fryer basket as your baking pan. The parchment paper circle that I instruct you to use while baking the cookies is simply to prevent the butter in the dough from dripping and smoking. You will also notice the majority of these cookie recipes require chilling the dough. Letting the dough chill prior to baking helps the butter to stay in a somewhat solid state, which means the cookies will spread less in the air fryer. A sturdier cookie is always good, so plan ahead with your prep time.

A word of caution: Please don't try and preheat your air fryer with the parchment paper circle already inside the basket. I learned the hard way that this means a smoky kitchen and a foul smell from burnt paper. Because I didn't even think to hold the parchment down with something (like, say, dried beans, the way we do when we blind-bake air fryer tarts), the paper was swept up in the air circulation and got caught in an upper crevice of the air fryer. Not fun! Don't worry about the parchment burning when baking the cookies though—the weight from the dough will keep the parchment in place, preventing it from coming into direct contact with the heat.

Some of my favorites from this chapter are the Dark Chocolate and Pistachio Cookies, Brown Butter Sugar Cookies, and you can't go wrong with Funfetti Sugar Cookies. With these recipes, it's my hope that I've made a strong, convincing case for the air fryer cookie.

Chocolate Chip Sea Salt Cookies

A perfectly sweet and salty cookie. I find sea salt in the spice aisle at my grocery store; you may also order online from Amazon or a specialty food store.

YIELD: 8 cookies   **PREP TIME:** 1 hour, 10 minutes (includes chilling)
COOK TIME: 16 minutes

½ cup plus 1 tablespoon all-purpose flour

¼ teaspoon baking soda

¼ teaspoon salt

¼ cup (½ stick) unsalted butter, at room temperature

¼ cup packed light brown sugar

2 tablespoons granulated sugar

1 large egg yolk

½ teaspoon vanilla extract

⅓ cup mini chocolate chips

1 teaspoon sea salt

TO MAKE THE COOKIES:

1. Trace an 8-inch circle onto a piece of parchment paper. Cut out the circle and set aside.

2. In a small bowl, whisk together the flour, baking soda, and salt to combine.

3. In the bowl of a stand mixer fitted with the paddle attachment, cream the butter, brown sugar, and granulated sugar on medium speed until fluffy, about 2 minutes. Add the egg yolk and vanilla extract and mix to combine.

4. Add the dry ingredients to the bowl of the stand mixer and mix on low speed until cookie dough forms. Fold in the mini chocolate chips.

5. Cover the bowl with plastic wrap and refrigerate for 1 hour.

6. After 1 hour, remove the cookie dough from the fridge and preheat your air fryer to 350°F for 10 minutes.

7. Use a cookie scoop to scoop 8 (1-inch) cookies onto a dinner plate or baking sheet. Using an oven mitt, carefully place the prepared parchment circle into the air fryer basket, and place 4 cookies on top of the parchment paper. Refrigerate the remaining 4 cookies while the first batch bakes.

8. Bake the first batch in the air fryer for 6 to 8 minutes, until cookies are golden brown and slightly crispy. Sprinkle the tops of each cookie with sea salt. Repeat with the remaining cookies and serve warm.

Brown Butter Sugar Cookies with Cinnamon Sugar

This is my number one, all-time favorite cookie. Brown butter is a gift on this earth, and I try to use it in as many dessert recipes as I can. Don't be intimidated if you've never browned butter before—I've written a clear guide in the recipe instructions below.

YIELD: 8 cookies **PREP TIME:** 1 hour, 5 minutes (includes chilling)
COOK TIME: 16 minutes

4½ tablespoons granulated sugar, divided

½ teaspoon ground cinnamon, divided

¼ cup (½ stick) unsalted butter

½ cup plus 2 tablespoons all-purpose flour

¼ teaspoon baking soda

¼ teaspoon salt

3½ tablespoons packed light brown sugar

1 large egg, at room temperature

½ teaspoon vanilla extract

TO MAKE THE COOKIES:

1. Trace an 8-inch circle onto a piece of parchment paper. Cut out the circle and set aside.

2. In a small bowl, whisk together 1 tablespoon of the granulated sugar with ¼ teaspoon of the cinnamon to combine. Set aside.

3. In a light-colored skillet set medium heat, melt the butter. Whisk occasionally as the butter begins to foam. After a couple of minutes, the butter will begin to brown—keep on whisking. After 5 to 7 minutes, the butter will turn deep brown in color and give off a nutty aroma. Remove from

heat, pour into the bowl of a stand mixer, and let cool for 5 minutes.

4. In a small bowl, whisk together the flour, baking soda, salt, and remaining ¼ teaspoon cinnamon to combine.

5. To the bowl of the stand mixer fitted with the paddle attachment, add the remaining granulated sugar and the brown sugar to the cooled brown butter and mix on medium-high speed for 2 minutes. Beat in the egg and vanilla extract.

6. Pour the dry ingredients into the bowl and mix on low speed to combine. Gradually increase the mixing speed until a somewhat greasy but firm cookie dough has formed.

7. Roll the dough into 8 balls and toss each in the prepared cinnamon sugar to coat. Set the dough balls on a dinner plate and refrigerate for 30 minutes.

8. Preheat your air fryer to 350°F for 10 minutes.

9. Using an oven mitt, carefully place the parchment paper circle into the air fryer basket. Remove the cookies from the refrigerator and bake 4 at a time on the parchment in your air fryer for 7 to 8 minutes, or until the cookies have browned.

Butterscotch Chip and Pretzel Cookies

I love the classic flavor combination of sweet and salty. The butterscotch and pretzels in these cookies balance each other out, creating a delicious bite. Cornstarch is used in this recipe as it helps to produce a chewy cookie, something I'm never mad about. Feel free to dot the tops of the cookies with any leftover pretzel pieces before baking them, which makes for pretty presentation as well as maximum pretzel flavor.

YIELD: 8 cookies   **PREP TIME:** 1 hour, 10 minutes (includes chilling)
COOK TIME: 16 minutes

1 cup all-purpose flour

1 teaspoon cornstarch

½ teaspoon baking soda

¼ teaspoon salt

6½ tablespoons unsalted butter, at room temperature

6 tablespoons packed light brown sugar

2 tablespoons granulated sugar

1 large egg, at room temperature

1 teaspoon vanilla extract

½ cup butterscotch chips

½ cup salted pretzels, broken into small pieces

TO MAKE THE COOKIES:

1. Trace an 8-inch circle onto a piece of parchment paper. Cut out the circle and set aside.

2. In a small bowl, whisk together the flour, cornstarch, baking soda, and salt to combine.

3. To the bowl of a stand mixer fitted with the paddle attachment, cream the butter on medium speed until light and fluffy, 1 to 2 minutes.

4. Add the brown sugar and granulated sugar to the creamed butter and mix until incorporated, about 2 minutes. Add the egg and vanilla extract, and mix just to combine.

5. Scrape down the sides of the bowl, and mix in the dry ingredients on low speed, gradually increasing speed as the cookie dough forms.

6. Fold in the butterscotch chips and the broken pretzel pieces to the dough. Cover the bowl in plastic wrap and refrigerate for 1 hour.

7. After 1 hour, remove the dough from the fridge and preheat your air fryer to 350°F for 10 minutes.

8. Using an oven mitt, carefully place the parchment paper circle into the air fryer basket.

9. Scoop out 4 cookies using a cookie scoop and bake 4 at a time on the parchment in your air fryer for 6 to 8 minutes, until the cookies are golden brown. Repeat with the remaining 4 cookies. Let cool completely before serving.

Cranberry and Chocolate Chip Slice-and-Bake Cookies

Slice-and-bake cookies used to intimidate me for some reason, so I'd never made them prior to this. I've realized the error of my ways; slice-and-bake recipes are the only cookies I want to make now. You will be baking these in three batches of four, unless of course you have a 5-quart air fryer. A drizzle of melted white chocolate would not only double the chocolate flavor, but would complement the dried cranberries.

YIELD: 1 dozen   **PREP TIME:** 4 hours, 15 minutes (includes chilling)
COOK TIME: 24 minutes

6 tablespoons unsalted butter, at room temperature

⅓ cup packed light brown sugar

1 large egg, at room temperature

½ teaspoon vanilla extract

1 cup all-purpose flour

⅛ teaspoon salt

½ cup mini chocolate chips

¼ cup dried cranberries, chopped

TO MAKE THE COOKIES:

1. Trace an 8-inch circle onto a piece of parchment paper. Cut out the circle and set aside.

2. In the bowl of a stand mixer fitted with the paddle attachment, cream the butter on medium speed until light and fluffy, 1 to 2 minutes.

3. Add the brown sugar and mix on medium-high speed until fully incorporated. Beat in the egg and vanilla extract on high speed. Scrape down the sides of the bowl as needed.

4. Add the flour and salt and beat on medium speed until fully incorporated. The dough will be pretty thick and a bit sticky. With the mixer set to high speed, mix the dough one last time to fully combine.

5. Fold in the mini chocolate chips and the chopped dried cranberries to combine.

6. Turn the dough out onto a lightly-floured surface and shape into an 8-inch log, about 2 inches in diameter. Wrap the dough tightly with plastic and refrigerate at least 4 hours, or overnight.

7. After chilling, preheat your air fryer to 350°F for 10 minutes. Remove the dough from the refrigerator and slice into 12 equally sized cookies.

8. Using an oven mitt, carefully place the parchment paper circle into the air fryer basket. Place 4 cookies on the parchment in the air fryer basket and bake for 6 to 8 minutes, until the edges are golden brown. Repeat with the remaining cookies. Let cool completely before serving.

Classic Snickerdoodles

Snickerdoodles are a top-five favorite cookie for me. I'm so glad they worked out in the air fryer because a dessert cookbook without a snickerdoodle recipe is incomplete, in my opinion.

YIELD: 1 dozen **PREP TIME:** 20 minutes **COOK TIME:** 24 minutes

½ cup plus 2 tablespoons granulated sugar, divided

1¾ teaspoons ground cinnamon, divided

1½ cups all-purpose flour

1 teaspoon cream of tartar

½ teaspoon baking soda

¼ teaspoon salt

½ cup (1 stick) unsalted butter, at room temperature

1 large egg, at room temperature

1 teaspoon vanilla extract

TO MAKE THE COOKIES:

1. Trace an 8-inch circle onto a piece of parchment paper. Cut out the circle and set aside.

2. In a small bowl, stir 2 tablespoons of the sugar and ½ teaspoon of the ground cinnamon to combine. Set aside.

3. Preheat your air fryer to 375°F for 10 minutes.

4. In a small bowl, whisk together the flour, cream of tartar, baking soda, remaining ground cinnamon, and salt to combine.

5. In the bowl of a stand mixer fitted with the paddle attachment, cream the butter on medium speed until light and fluffy, 1 to 2 minutes. Add the remaining sugar and continue mixing until fully incorporated with the butter. Crack the egg into the bowl, and pour in the vanilla extract. Mix on medium speed to combine.

6. Add the dry ingredients to the bowl of the stand mixer and mix on low speed to combine.

7. Roll the dough into balls, about 1½ to 2 tablespoons in size, and roll each in the reserved cinnamon-sugar mixture.

8. Using an oven mitt, carefully place the parchment paper circle into the air fryer basket. Bake the cookies in batches of 4 for 6 to 8 minutes, or until cookies have browned slightly. The cookies will firm up slightly as they come to room temperature.

White Chocolate Macadamia Cookies

This is another of my all-time favorite cookies. In writing this cookbook, I've learned much about myself. I've found that I love a salty component in sweet desserts, and this classic cookie utilizes the wonderful saltiness of macadamia nuts.

YIELD: about 1 dozen   PREP TIME: 45 minutes (includes chilling)
COOK TIME: 30 minutes

1 cup plus 2 tablespoons all-purpose flour

¼ teaspoon baking soda

¼ teaspoon salt

6 tablespoon unsalted butter, at room temperature

½ cup light brown sugar

¼ cup granulated sugar

1 large egg, at room temperature

1 teaspoon vanilla extract

6 tablespoons white chocolate chips

6 tablespoons chopped macadamia nuts

TO MAKE THE COOKIES:

1. Trace an 8-inch circle onto a piece of parchment paper. Cut out the circle and set aside.

2. In a small bowl, whisk together the flour, baking soda, and salt to combine.

3. In the bowl of a stand mixer fitted with the paddle attachment, cream the butter, brown sugar, and granulated sugar on medium speed for 1 to 2 minutes. Add the egg and vanilla and continue mixing.

4. Gradually add the dry ingredients to the bowl and mix on low speed until a dough forms.

Fold in the white chocolate chips and the macadamia nuts.

5. Cover the bowl with plastic wrap. Refrigerate for at least 30 minutes.

6. Once chilled, preheat your air fryer to 325°F for 10 minutes.

7. Using an oven mitt, carefully place the prepared parchment circle into the air fryer basket. Scoop out 4 cookies using a cookie scoop and place onto the parchment circle, and bake for 8 to 10 minutes, until golden brown. Let cool completely before serving.

Funfetti Sugar Cookies

I know 15 cookies is an odd yield, but who will turn their nose up at those three extra cookies? You'll need to bake these cookies in three batches of four, then one last batch of three—four batches total. If that sounds like a lot, I'm here to encourage you. You can do it—and then you get to eat funfetti sugar cookies.

YIELD: 15 cookies **PREP TIME:** 1 hour, 20 minutes (includes chilling)
COOK TIME: 30 minutes

1½ cups all-purpose flour

¼ teaspoon salt

1 teaspoon baking powder

½ teaspoon baking soda

1 teaspoon cream of tartar

½ cup (1 stick) unsalted butter, at room temperature

¾ cup granulated sugar

1 large egg, at room temperature

1 teaspoon vanilla extract

½ cup rainbow sprinkles

TO MAKE THE COOKIES:

1. Trace an 8-inch circle onto a piece of parchment paper. Cut out the circle and set aside.

2. In a medium bowl, whisk together the flour, salt, baking powder, baking soda, and cream of tartar to combine.

3. In the bowl of a stand mixer fitted with the paddle attachment, cream the butter on medium speed until light and fluffy, 1 to 2 minutes. Add the sugar and continue mixing.

4. Mix in the egg and vanilla extract, and scrape down the sides of the bowl as needed.

5. Gradually add the dry ingredients to the bowl and mix well on low speed. Fold in the sprinkles.

6. Roll the cookie dough into balls using about 1 to 1½ tablespoons of dough each, and place the cookies on a small baking sheet or large dinner plate. Refrigerate for at least 1 hour.

7. Once chilled, preheat your air fryer to 350°F for 10 minutes.

8. Using an oven mitt, carefully place the prepared parchment circle into the air fryer basket. Place 4 cookies on top of the parchment paper and bake for 6 to 7 minutes, or until cookies have browned slightly and the centers have firmed.

9. Let the cookies cool completely before serving.

Dark Chocolate Pistachio Cookies

If it's possible for a cookie to be considered "sexy," I'm almost embarrassed to say I would refer to these luscious dark chocolate pistachio cookies as just that. Sometimes you just want adult flavors in a cookie, and this recipe fits the bill nicely. Feel free to drizzle melted dark chocolate over these once they have cooled.

YIELD: 1 dozen   **PREP TIME:** 1 hour, 15 minutes (includes chilling)
COOK TIME: 24 minutes

1 cup all-purpose flour

1 teaspoon cornstarch

½ teaspoon baking soda

¼ teaspoon salt

6 tablespoons unsalted butter, at room temperature

6 tablespoons packed light brown sugar

2 tablespoons granulated sugar

1 large egg, at room temperature

1 teaspoon vanilla extract

6 tablespoons dark chocolate chips

¼ cup unsalted pistachios, shelled and finely chopped

TO MAKE THE COOKIES:

1. Trace an 8-inch circle onto a piece of parchment paper. Cut out the circle and set aside.

2. In a small bowl, whisk the flour, cornstarch, baking soda, and salt to combine.

3. In the bowl of a stand mixer fitted with the paddle attachment, cream the butter on medium speed until light and fluffy, 1 to 2 minutes. Add the brown sugar and granulated sugar to the bowl and continue mixing until fully incorporated. Mix in the egg and vanilla extract and scrape down the sides of the bowl as needed.

4. Gradually add the dry ingredients to the bowl and mix on low speed to combine. Fold in the dark chocolate chips and finely chopped pistachios and mix by hand to combine.

5. Using a cookie scoop, scoop out 12 balls of dough and place on a dinner plate. Cover the plate with plastic wrap and refrigerate for at least 1 hour.

6. Once chilled, remove the cookies from the refrigerator and preheat your air fryer to 350°F for 10 minutes.

7. Using an oven mitt, carefully place the prepared parchment circle into the air fryer basket.

8. Place 4 cookies on top of the parchment paper and bake for 6 to 8 minutes, until the cookies are golden brown. Repeat with the remaining cookies. Let cool completely before serving.

Peanut Butter Cookies

These classic cookies don't need an introduction, really. One note: Don't use crunchy or chunky peanut butter for these, as the extra nuts will throw off the texture. And a recommendation: If you're making these in the colder months, add ½ teaspoon ground cinnamon with the rest of the dry ingredients. The warmth of the cinnamon pairs very well with the sweet and salty peanut butter.

YIELD: 15 cookies   **PREP TIME:** 1 hour, 10 minutes (includes chilling)
COOK TIME: 32 minutes

1½ cups plus 1 tablespoon all-purpose flour

½ teaspoon baking soda

½ teaspoon baking powder

¼ teaspoon salt

½ cup (1 stick) unsalted butter, at room temperature

½ cup granulated sugar

6 tablespoons packed light brown sugar

1 large egg, at room temperature

1 teaspoon vanilla extract

½ cup creamy peanut butter

TO MAKE THE COOKIES:

1. Trace an 8-inch circle onto a piece of parchment paper. Cut out the circle and set aside.

2. In a small bowl, whisk together the flour, baking soda, baking powder, and salt to combine.

3. In the bowl of a stand mixer fitted with the paddle attachment, cream the butter, granulated sugar, and brown sugar on medium speed until light and fluffy, 1 to 2 minutes.

4. Add the egg and continue mixing until combined. Scrape down the sides of the bowl as needed. Add the vanilla extract and peanut butter, and mix until very well combined.

5. Gradually pour the dry ingredients into the bowl and mix on low speed until well combined. The dough will be thick.

6. Roll balls of the dough into 15 equally sized pieces, about 1½ to 2 tablespoons for each cookie, and place onto a dinner plate or small cookie sheet. Using a fork, press a crisscross pattern into the top of each cookie. Refrigerate for at least 1 hour.

7. Once chilled, preheat your air fryer to 350°F for 10 minutes.

8. Using an oven mitt, carefully place the prepared parchment circle into the air fryer basket. Place 4 cookies on top of the parchment paper and bake for 7 to 8 minutes or until golden brown. Repeat with the remaining cookies. Let cool completely before serving.

Brown Sugar and Walnut Cookies

This recipe's yield depends on the size of your cookie scoop or spoon. The larger the cookie scoop or spoon, the fewer cookies this dough will give you. I got exactly 12 cookies using a tablespoon as a scoop, so that's what I recommend you do. To toast the walnuts, set a dry skillet over medium heat and add the nuts. Stir the nuts and swirl the pan to ensure even toasting. The nuts are done when they've browned slightly and, you guessed it, have given off a nutty aroma, about 5 minutes or so for 1½ tablespoons of walnuts. No need to dirty your stand mixer for this—the butter for these cookies is melted, making this recipe one-bowl.

YIELD: 10 to 12 cookies   **PREP TIME:** 1 hour, 15 minutes (includes chilling)
COOK TIME: 24 to 32 minutes

1 cup all-purpose flour

½ teaspoon baking soda

½ teaspoon cornstarch

⅛ teaspoon salt

½ teaspoon ground cinnamon

6 tablespoons unsalted butter, melted

½ cup plus 2 tablespoons packed light brown sugar

1 large egg, at room temperature

1 teaspoon vanilla extract

1/4 cup whole walnuts, toasted and chopped

1 tablespoon granulated sugar, for rolling

TO MAKE THE COOKIES:

1. Trace an 8-inch circle onto a piece of parchment paper. Cut out the circle and set aside.

2. In a large bowl, whisk together the flour, baking soda, cornstarch, ground cinnamon, and salt to combine.

3. In a medium bowl, whisk the melted butter and brown sugar very well. Whisk in the egg, then whisk in the vanilla extract. Pour the wet ingredients into the dry ingredients and stir to incorporate. The dough will be thick. Fold in the chopped toasted walnuts.

4. Using either a cookie scoop or a tablespoon, scoop pieces of the dough and roll into equally sized balls. Roll the cookies in the granulated sugar and place on a large dinner plate. Refrigerate for at least 1 hour.

5. Once chilled, preheat your air fryer to 325°F for 10 minutes.

6. Using an oven mitt, carefully place the prepared parchment circle into the air fryer basket. Place 4 cookies onto the parchment paper and bake for 8 minutes, or until golden brown. Repeat with the remaining cookies. Let cool completely before serving.

Dark Chocolate Cookies

I'm a fan of all chocolate, but especially dark chocolate. Make these for the dark chocolate lover in your life.

YIELD: 8 **PREP TIME:** 3 hours, 30 minutes (includes chilling)
COOK TIME: 16 minutes

½ cup all-purpose flour

2 tablespoons plus 2 teaspoons unsweetened Dutch-process cocoa powder

2 tablespoons plus 2 teaspoons dark cocoa powder

½ teaspoon baking soda

pinch of salt

¼ cup (½ stick) unsalted butter, at room temperature

¼ cup granulated sugar

¼ cup packed light brown sugar

1 large egg, at room temperature

½ teaspoon vanilla extract

1 tablespoon whole milk

¼ cup dark chocolate chips

TO MAKE THE COOKIES:

1. Trace an 8-inch circle onto a piece of parchment paper. Cut out the circle and set aside.

2. In a medium bowl, whisk together the flour, unsweetened Dutch-process cocoa powder, dark cocoa powder, baking soda, and salt to combine.

3. In the bowl of a stand mixer fitted with the paddle attachment and set to medium speed, cream the butter for 1 minute. Add the granulated sugar and brown sugar, and continue mixing. Add the egg and mix well, scraping down the sides of the bowl as needed. Add the vanilla extract and mix well.

4. Add the dry ingredients to the bowl on low speed. Pour in the milk and continue to mix. The batter will be thick and may be sticky. Stir in the dark chocolate chips by hand.

5. Cover the bowl with plastic wrap and refrigerate for at least 3 hours.

6. Once the dough has been chilled, set it on your counter for 30 minutes to allow it to come back to room temperature slightly.

7. Preheat your air fryer to 350°F for 10 minutes while you roll the dough into cookies.

8. Roll the dough into 8 (1-inch) cookies using either a cookie scoop or a tablespoon.

9. Using an oven mitt, carefully place the prepared parchment circle into the air fryer basket. Place 4 cookies on top of the parchment paper and bake for 8 minutes, or until the cookies have crisped slightly around the edges. Repeat for the remaining cookies. Let cool completely before serving.

Easiest Christmas Cookies

These are made with store-bought cookie dough mix, as I wanted to just see how they would work out in the air fryer. Unsurprisingly, they did! Decorate these however you wish. I used a combination of white and milk chocolate to dip the cookies into once baked and cooled. Add Christmas sprinkles on top and you're good to go to your next holiday party.

YIELD: 12   **PREP TIME:** 10 minutes   **COOK TIME:** 20 minutes

1 (7.5-ounce) pouch chocolate chip cookie mix

¼ cup white chocolate, melted

¼ cup semisweet milk chocolate, melted

Christmas sprinkles

TO MAKE THE COOKIES:

1. Trace an 8-inch circle onto a piece of parchment paper. Cut out the circle and set aside.

2. Preheat your air fryer to the temperature indicated on the cookie mix, probably 350°F.

3. Prepare cookies as instructed on the cookie mix. Using an oven mitt, carefully place the prepared parchment circle into the air fryer basket. Place 4 cookies on top of the parchment and bake for 6 to 7 minutes. Repeat with remaining cookies. Let cool completely before decorating.

4. In two small bowls, pour the melted white and milk chocolates.

5. Line a cookie sheet with parchment paper. Dunk each cookie into either of the melted chocolates and top with Christmas sprinkles. Lay on the prepared cookie sheet and let the chocolate harden before serving.

Red Velvet Cookies

Red velvet cake in cookie form—you can't really go wrong with that.

YIELD: 8 **PREP TIME:** 1 hour, 10 minutes (includes chilling)
COOK TIME: 18 minutes

¾ cup all-purpose flour

2 tablespoons unsweetened Dutch-process cocoa powder

½ teaspoon baking soda

⅛ teaspoon salt

¼ cup (½ stick) unsalted butter, at room temperature

6 tablespoons packed light brown sugar

2 tablespoons granulated sugar

1 large egg, at room temperature

½ tablespoon whole milk

1 teaspoon vanilla extract

½ tablespoon red gel food coloring

½ cup semisweet chocolate chips

TO MAKE THE COOKIES:

1. Trace an 8-inch circle onto a piece of parchment paper. Cut out the circle and set aside.

2. In a medium bowl, whisk together the flour, cocoa powder, baking soda, and salt to combine.

3. In the bowl of a stand mixer fitted with the paddle attachment, cream the butter on medium speed for 1 minute. Add the brown sugar and granulated sugar, and continue to mix until fluffy, 3 to 4 minutes. Add the egg, milk, and vanilla extract and mix, scraping down the sides of the bowl as needed. Add the red food coloring and mix on low speed until combined.

4. Add the dry ingredients to the bowl on low speed and mix. Stir in the chocolate chips by hand. Cover the bowl with plastic wrap and refrigerate for 1 hour.

5. Once chilled, preheat your air fryer to 350°F for 10 minutes.

6. Roll the dough into 8 (1-inch) cookies using a cookie scoop or tablespoon. Using an oven mitt, carefully place the prepared parchment circle into the air fryer basket. Place 4 cookies on top of the parchment and bake for 9 minutes, or until the cookies have slightly crisped around the edges. Repeat with the remaining cookies.

7. Let cool completely before serving.

Peanut Butter Chip Cookies

You can find peanut butter chips in the baking aisle at your grocery store. Once you do, you are very close to being able to eat these delicious peanut butter cookies.

YIELD: 8   **PREP TIME:** 16 minutes   **COOK TIME:** 20 minutes

⅔ cup all-purpose flour

¼ teaspoon baking soda

¼ teaspoon baking powder

⅛ teaspoon salt

½ cup packed light brown sugar

¼ cup creamy peanut butter

¼ cup (½ stick) unsalted butter, at room temperature

1 large egg, at room temperature

½ cup peanut butter chips

TO MAKE THE COOKIES:

1. Trace an 8-inch circle onto a piece of parchment paper. Cut out the circle and set aside.

2. Preheat your air fryer to 375°F for 10 minutes.

3. In a small bowl, whisk together the flour, baking soda, baking powder, and salt to combine.

4. In the bowl of a stand mixer fitted with the paddle attachment, mix the brown sugar, peanut butter, butter, and egg on medium speed until creamy.

5. Add the dry ingredients on low speed until combined. Stir in the peanut butter chips by hand.

6. Roll the dough into 1½-inch balls using a cookie scoop or tablespoon. Using an oven mitt, carefully place the prepared parchment circle into the air fryer basket. Place 4 cookies on top of the parchment paper and bake for 6 to 8 minutes, or until the cookies have crisped slightly around the edges. Repeat with the remaining cookies.

7. Let cool before serving.

Double Chocolate Hazelnut Cookies

Maximum chocolate flavor can be found in these cookies, which are enhanced by buttery hazelnuts.

YIELD: 8   **PREP TIME:** 14 minutes   **COOK TIME:** 20 minutes

⅔ cup all-purpose flour

¼ teaspoon baking soda

⅛ teaspoon sea salt

3½ tablespoons unsweetened Dutch-process cocoa powder

¼ cup (½ stick) unsalted butter, at room temperature

¼ cup granulated sugar

¼ cup packed light brown sugar

1 large egg, at room temperature

¼ teaspoon vanilla extract

¼ cup semisweet chocolate chips

¼ cup hazelnuts, chopped

TO MAKE THE COOKIES:

1. Trace an 8-inch circle onto a piece of parchment paper. Cut out the circle and set aside.

2. Preheat your air fryer to 350°F for 10 minutes.

3. In a medium bowl, whisk together the flour, baking soda, sea salt, and cocoa powder to combine.

4. In the bowl of a stand mixer fitted with the paddle attachment, cream the butter on medium speed for 1 minute. Add the granulated sugar and brown sugar, and continue to mix. Crack in the egg and add the vanilla extract. Mix well, scraping down the sides of the bowl as needed.

5. Add the dry ingredients to the bowl and mix on low speed. Stir in the chocolate chips and chopped hazelnuts by hand.

6. Using an oven mitt, carefully place the prepared parchment circle into the air fryer basket. Place 4 cookies on top of the parchment and bake for 6 to 7 minutes, or until the cookies have crisped slightly around the edges. Repeat with the remaining cookies.

7. Let cool completely before serving.

Ginger Cookies

My boyfriend and I have a ginger cat named Ginger, so I had her on my brain when I thought about how to adapt these cookies for the air fryer. These would be a good treat to bring along to any Thanksgiving or Christmas parties, as the warmth from the ginger makes them festive.

YIELD: 6   **PREP TIME:** 30 minutes (includes chilling)   **COOK TIME:** 20 minutes

1¼ cups all-purpose flour

1 teaspoon baking soda

¼ teaspoon salt

½ tablespoon ground ginger

¼ teaspoon ground allspice

6 tablespoons unsalted butter, at room temperature

¼ cup packed light brown sugar

¼ cup granulated sugar

3 tablespoons molasses

1 large egg, at room temperature

TO MAKE THE COOKIES:

1. Trace an 8-inch circle onto a piece of parchment paper. Cut out the circle and set aside.

2. Preheat your air fryer to 350°F for 10 minutes.

3. In a medium bowl, whisk together the flour, baking soda, salt, ginger, and allspice to combine.

4. In the bowl of a stand mixer fitted with the paddle attachment, cream together the butter, brown sugar, and granulated sugar until very light and fluffy, 3 to 4 minutes. Add the molasses and egg and mix very well, scraping down the sides of the bowl as needed.

5. Add the dry ingredients to the bowl and mix on low speed. Turn the dough out onto your counter and flatten it into a disk. Cover with plastic wrap and refrigerate for 20 minutes.

6. Roll the dough into 6 (1-inch) cookies using a cookie scoop or tablespoon.

7. Using an oven mitt, carefully place the prepared parchment circle into the air fryer basket. Place 3 cookies on top of the parchment and bake for 9 to 10 minutes, or until the cookies have crisped slightly around the edges. Repeat with the remaining cookies.

8. Let cool completely before serving.

Chocolate Cherry Cookies

I know I've said this about many of the flavor combinations found in this book, but chocolate and cherry really is my favorite too! After baking and eating these cookies, I hope you'll feel the same.

YIELD: 16   **PREP TIME:** 10 minutes   **COOK TIME:** 32 minutes

1¼ cups all-purpose flour

½ teaspoon baking soda

¼ teaspoon salt

6 tablespoons unsweetened Dutch-process cocoa powder

½ cup (1 stick) unsalted butter, at room temperature

½ cup granulated sugar

½ cup packed light brown sugar

1 large egg, at room temperature

½ teaspoon vanilla extract

¼ cup chocolate chips

¼ cup dried cherries

TO MAKE THE COOKIES:

1. Trace an 8-inch circle onto a piece of parchment paper. Cut out the circle and set aside.

2. Preheat your air fryer to 350°F for 10 minutes.

3. In a medium bowl, whisk together the flour, baking soda, salt, and cocoa powder to combine.

4. In the bowl of a stand mixer fitted with the paddle attachment, cream the butter, granulated sugar, and brown sugar on medium speed until very fluffy, 3 to 4 minutes. Add the egg and vanilla extract, and continue to mix, scraping down the sides of the bowl as needed.

5. Add the dry ingredients to the bowl and mix on low speed. Stir in the chocolate chips and dried cherries by hand.

6. Using an oven mitt, carefully place the prepared parchment circle into the air fryer basket. Using a cookie scoop or tablespoon, drop 3 or 4 cookies on top of the parchment and bake in the air fryer for 7 to 8 minutes, or until the cookies have crisped slightly around the edges. Repeat with the remaining cookies.

7. Let cool completely before serving.

Chocolate Golden Raisin Cookies

If you've never tried golden raisins before, you're in for a treat. The raisins have a tart, slightly tangy flavor profile, making them pair nicely with the semisweet chocolate chips.

YIELD: 18 **PREP TIME:** 10 minutes **COOK TIME:** 24 minutes

¾ cup all-purpose flour

½ teaspoon baking soda

½ teaspoon salt

½ cup (1 stick) unsalted butter, at room temperature

6 tablespoons packed light brown sugar

6 tablespoons granulated sugar

1 large egg, at room temperature

½ teaspoon vanilla extract

1 cup rolled oats

¾ cup golden raisins

¼ cup semisweet chocolate chips

TO MAKE THE COOKIES:

1. Trace an 8-inch circle onto a piece of parchment paper. Cut out the circle and set aside.

2. Preheat your air fryer to 375°F for 10 minutes.

3. In a medium bowl, whisk together the flour, baking soda, and salt to combine.

4. In the bowl of a stand mixer fitted with the paddle attachment, cream the butter, brown sugar, and granulated sugar on medium speed until very fluffy, 3 to 4 minutes. Crack in the egg and add the vanilla extract and mix, scraping down the sides of the bowl as needed. Stir in the rolled oats, golden raisins, and chocolate chips by hand.

5. Using an oven mitt, carefully place the prepared parchment circle into the air fryer basket. Using a cookie scoop or a tablespoon, drop 3 or 4 cookies on top of the parchment and bake for 5 to 6 minutes, until golden brown. Repeat with the remaining cookies.

6. Let cool slightly before serving.

Mint Chocolate Chip Cookies

There are a couple of mint-chocolate combinations in this book, but these cookies belong center stage. Steeping the mint leaves into the milk takes these cookies to another level.

YIELD: 6   **PREP TIME:** 1 hour, 40 minutes (includes chilling)
COOK TIME: 20 minutes

¼ cup (½ stick) unsalted butter

¼ cup fresh mint, roughly chopped

¾ cup all-purpose flour

½ teaspoon baking soda

¼ teaspoon salt

¼ cup packed light brown sugar

¼ cup granulated sugar

1 large egg, at room temperature

½ teaspoon vanilla extract

¼ cup semisweet chocolate chips

TO MAKE THE COOKIES:

1. Trace an 8-inch circle with onto a piece of parchment paper. Cut out the circle and set aside.

2. In a small saucepan set on medium heat, melt the butter and chopped mint leaves. Once you begin to smell the mint, 1 to 2 minutes, remove from the heat and steep for 20 minutes. Pour the mixture through a fine-mesh sieve and set aside.

3. In a small bowl, whisk the flour, baking soda, and salt to combine.

4. In the bowl of a stand mixer fitted with the paddle attachment, cream the butter, brown sugar, and granulated sugar on medium speed until fluffy, 3 to 4 minutes. Add the egg and vanilla extract and continue to mix, scraping down the sides of the bowl as needed.

5. Add the dry ingredients to the bowl and mix on low speed. Stir in the chocolate chips by hand and cover the bowl with plastic wrap. Refrigerate for 1 hour.

6. Once chilled, preheat your air fryer to 350°F for 10 minutes.

7. Roll the dough into 1-inch cookies using a cookie scoop or tablespoon. Using an oven mitt, carefully place the prepared parchment circle into the air fryer basket. Place 3 cookies on top of the parchment and bake for 7 to 8 minutes, or until the cookies have crisped slightly around the edges. Repeat with the remaining cookies.

8. Let cool slightly before serving.

DONUTS

Your mileage may vary when it comes to the air fryer donut. What I mean by that is these recipes are guidelines, and since my air fryer may not be the same version you have at home, you may need to adjust baking time. For most of these donut recipes, I'm setting baking time at 375°F for about 6 to 7 minutes, and about 3 to 4 minutes for donut holes. But again, test the bake time with your brand of air fryer by just simply baking one donut at first. Since my air fryer is 3 quarts and therefore on the smaller side as far as air fryers go, I was only able to fry two donuts at a time. However, if you have a mini donut cutter, as well as one of the 5-quart air fryers, you can easily fry up lots of donuts relatively quickly.

I used an Ateco brand 3½-inch donut cutter, but if you have a cookie cutter of the same size and a standard-sized pastry tip, you can use both to make your donut shape. A mini donut cutter also works and will yield many more donuts. For these, we are sticking with our trusty parchment paper circle, as we did to make air fryer cookies. The only other special equipment you'll need is a digital thermometer. We aren't frying the donuts in oil, so you'll only need the thermometer to make sure the milk's temperature is correct. Letting the donuts rest (and rise) before baking ensures a lighter dough, which means you shouldn't skip this step. Almost all of these recipes use the first, "master" air fryer donut recipe as a base. From there, we build flavors using delicious glazes, fillings, and spices.

Vanilla Glazed Donuts

A simple donut made delicious with good ingredients. The air fryer donut is something I wish every donut lover could try!

YIELD: 6   **PREP TIME:** 1 hour, 40 minutes   **COOK TIME:** 18 minutes

DONUTS:

½ cup whole milk, warmed to 110°F

½ tablespoon active dry yeast

2 tablespoons granulated sugar, divided

1 large egg

3 tablespoons unsalted butter, melted and cooled

½ teaspoon vanilla extract

2 cups all-purpose flour, divided, plus more for dusting and rolling

¼ teaspoon salt

GLAZE:

1 cup confectioners' sugar, sifted

2 tablespoons plus 2 teaspoons heavy cream

¼ teaspoon vanilla extract

TO MAKE THE DONUTS:

1. Trace an 8-inch circle onto a piece of parchment paper. Cut out the circle and set aside.

2. Pour the warmed milk into the bowl of a stand mixer fitted with the dough hook attachment. Sprinkle in the yeast and ¼ teaspoon of the sugar on top of the milk. Stir with a spoon and let sit for 5 minutes or until the yeast has foamed and become frothy.

3. With the mixer set to low speed, add the remaining sugar, the egg, butter, vanilla, 1 cup of flour, and salt. Mix on low speed for about 1 minute to combine. Add the remaining flour and mix on medium-high speed until the

dough begins to pull away from the sides of the bowl. This dough will be thick and somewhat sticky.

4. With your hands, form dough into a ball and turn out onto a lightly floured surface. Knead dough for 2 minutes and place into a greased bowl.

5. Cover the bowl with plastic wrap and let it rest and rise in a warm environment until doubled in size, 1 to 1½ hours.

6. Once properly rested and doubled in size, punch the dough down with your fist to release air bubbles. Turn out the dough onto a lightly floured surface. Roll the dough out to about ½ inch thick. Using a donut cutter, cut out 6 donuts.

7. Place the donuts on a small baking sheet lined with parchment paper. Cover with a kitchen towel and let rest for 10 minutes while you preheat your air fryer.

8. Preheat your air fryer to 375°F for 10 minutes.

9. Using an oven mitt, carefully place the prepared parchment circle into the air fryer basket. Place 2 donuts on the parchment and fry for 3 to 4 minutes, then rotate the donuts 180 degrees to ensure even frying. Fry for an additional 2 minutes, or until completely golden brown.

10. Make the glaze while the first batch is frying, and whisk all of the ingredients together in a medium bowl.

11. Remove the donuts from the air fryer and let cool on a cooling rack just slightly before glazing.

12. To glaze, dip each donut into the glaze, making sure to cover all sides. Place back on the cooling rack to let the glaze dry. Repeat with the remaining donuts.

Chocolate Glazed Donuts

The glaze on these guys is very chocolatey. The reason we sift the confectioners' sugar for the glaze is to ensure a shiny, smooth consistency. Practically a hallmark in this classic donut.

YIELD: 6 **PREP TIME:** 1 hour, 40 minutes **COOK TIME:** 18 minutes

DONUTS:

½ cup whole milk, warmed to 110°F

½ tablespoon active dry yeast

2 tablespoons granulated sugar, divided

1 large egg

3 tablespoons unsalted butter, melted and cooled

½ teaspoon vanilla extract

2 cups all-purpose flour, divided plus more for dusting and rolling

¼ teaspoon salt

GLAZE:

¾ cup confectioners' sugar, sifted

2 tablespoons unsweetened Dutch-process cocoa powder

1 tablespoon whole milk

1 teaspoon vanilla extract

TO MAKE THE DONUTS:

1. Trace an 8-inch circle onto a piece of parchment paper. Cut out the circle and set aside.

2. Pour the warmed milk into the bowl of a stand mixer fitted with the dough hook attachment. Sprinkle in the yeast and ¼ teaspoon of the sugar on top of the milk. Stir with a spoon and let sit for 5 minutes or until the yeast has foamed and become frothy.

3. With the mixer set to low speed, add the remaining sugar, the egg, butter, vanilla, 1 cup of flour, and salt. Mix on low speed for about 1 minute to combine.

Add the remaining flour and mix on medium-high speed until the dough begins to pull away from the sides of the bowl. This dough will be thick and somewhat sticky.

4. With your hands, form dough into a ball and turn out onto a lightly floured surface. Knead dough for 2 minutes and place into a greased bowl.

5. Cover the bowl with plastic wrap and let it rest and rise in a warm environment until doubled in size, 1 to 1½ hours.

6. Once properly rested and doubled in size, punch the dough down with your fist to release air bubbles. Turn out the dough onto a lightly floured surface. Roll the dough out to about ½ inch thick. Using a donut cutter, cut out 6 donuts.

7. Place the donuts on a small baking sheet lined with parchment paper. Cover with a kitchen towel and let rest for 10 minutes while you preheat your air fryer.

8. Preheat your air fryer to 375°F for 10 minutes.

9. Using an oven mitt, carefully place the prepared parchment circle into the air fryer basket.

Place 2 donuts on the parchment and fry for 3 to 4 minutes, then rotate the donuts 180 degrees to ensure even frying. Fry for an additional 2 minutes, or until completely golden brown.

10. Make the glaze while the first batch is frying, and whisk all of the ingredients together in a medium bowl.

11. Remove the donuts from the air fryer and let cool on a cooling rack just slightly before glazing.

12. To glaze, dip each donut into the glaze, making sure to cover all sides. Place back on the cooling rack to let the glaze dry. Repeat with the remaining donuts.

Cake Donuts with Brown Butter Glaze

A cake donut is simply a donut that gets its rise from baking powder instead of yeast. There's still about an hour and a half prep time though, because the dough also needs to chill. Don't forget, donuts are a labor of love. You can either freeze your donut holes from this, or fry them up as well. Recommended frying time for donut holes is around 1 to 2 minutes at 350°F degrees, but times for your air fryer may differ.

YIELD: 6 **PREP TIME:** 1 hour, 20 minutes **COOK TIME:** 18 minutes

DONUTS:
1¾ cups all-purpose flour

½ tablespoon baking powder

½ teaspoon ground cinnamon

pinch of salt

½ cup granulated sugar

1 large egg, at room temperature

½ teaspoon vanilla extract

½ teaspoon lemon zest
(from 1 small lemon)

2½ tablespoons unsalted butter, melted

½ cup sour cream, at room temperature

GLAZE:
1½ cups confectioners' sugar, sifted

1½ tablespoons unsalted butter, browned and cooled (page 10)

¼ teaspoon vanilla extract

1½ to 2 tablespoons whole milk

TO MAKE THE DONUTS:

1. Trace an 8-inch circle onto a piece of parchment paper. Cut out the circle and set aside.

2. In a large bowl, whisk together the flour, baking powder, cinnamon, and salt to combine. Make a well in the center.

3. In a medium bowl, whisk the granulated sugar, egg, vanilla extract, and lemon zest very

well to combine. Slowly pour in the melted butter and stir to incorporate. Spoon half of the sour cream into the bowl, and mix well. Repeat with the remaining sour cream. Mix until completely combined.

4. Using a rubber spatula, fold the wet ingredients into the well of the dry ingredients; combine well.

5. Turn dough out onto a lightly floured surface and give the dough 1 or 2 kneads, just to pull it together. Cover the dough with plastic wrap and refrigerate for at least 1 hour.

6. Once dough has chilled, preheat your air fryer to 375°F for 10 minutes. Turn the dough out onto a lightly floured surface and sprinkle additional flour on top.

7. Roll dough out to about ½ inch thick. Using a donut cutter, cut out 6 donuts.

8. Using an oven mitt, carefully place the prepared parchment circle into the air fryer basket. Place 3 donuts on the parchment paper and fry for 3 to 4 minutes. Rotate the donuts 180 degrees to ensure even frying, then fry for an additional 2 minutes, or until completely golden brown.

9. Make the glaze while the first batch is frying, and whisk all of the ingredients together in a medium bowl.

10. Remove donuts from air fryer and let cool just slightly on a cooling rack before glazing.

11. To glaze, dip each donut into the glaze, making sure to cover the top of the donut completely. Place back on the cooling rack to let the glaze dry. Repeat with the remaining donuts.

Apricot Jam-Filled Almond Sugar Brown Butter Donuts

The longest recipe title in existence, maybe, but so necessary. I found inspiration for these donuts at home in the West. Apricots are a native to Central California, where I grew up, where my roots were first planted. My grandparents live in Apricot Central, a small town called Patterson about an hour and a half east of San Francisco. There, apricots grow in abundance, as if Patterson were the only place on the earth where apricots could even exist. The fruit is featured in this donut alongside almonds, making for a classically sweet-salty combination. Eat these as I did, with fervor.

YIELD: 6   **PREP TIME:** 2 hours, 20 minutes   **COOK TIME:** 18 minutes

DONUTS:

½ cup whole milk, warmed to 100°F

2 tablespoons plus 2 teaspoons granulated sugar, divided

½ (.25-ounce) package active dry yeast

1 large egg yolk, at room temperature

2 tablespoons unsalted butter, browned, cooled, and solidified (page 10)

1⅔ to 1¾ cups all-purpose flour

¼ teaspoon ground cinnamon

¼ teaspoon salt

½ cup whole almonds, toasted and chopped

¼ to ½ cup apricot jam

ALMOND SUGAR:

¾ cups granulated sugar

½ teaspoon almond extract

TO MAKE THE DONUTS:

1. Trace an 8-inch circle onto a piece of parchment paper. Cut out the circle and set aside.

2. In the bowl of a stand mixer fitted with the dough hook attachment, pour the warmed milk, 1 tablespoon of granulated sugar, and the yeast, and stir just to combine. Let the mixture sit until the yeast has foamed and become frothy.

3. To the bowl of the stand mixer, add the egg yolk and the remaining sugar and beat on low speed to combine. Drop the room-temperature solidified brown butter into the bowl in chunks and continue mixing until the butter is incorporated.

4. To the bowl of the stand mixer, add 1 cup of the flour, and all of the cinnamon and salt, and continue mixing on low speed until the flour has been incorporated. Add another ⅔ cup of flour and mix to combine.

5. With the mixer on high speed, mix the dough for a good 5 minutes until it is elastic-looking and smooth. Add additional flour by the tablespoon if the dough is too sticky, making sure to add no more than a total of 1¾ cups flour.

6. Turn the dough out onto a lightly floured surface, knead for another couple of minutes, and shape into a ball. Transfer the dough to a greased bowl and cover with bowl plastic wrap. Let the dough rise in a warm environment for 1½ hours, or until doubled in size.

7. Punch down the dough after it has risen and turn out onto a lightly floured surface. Roll out the dough out into a circle about ½ inch thick. Using a 3-inch cookie cutter, cut out 6 donuts.

8. Place the donuts onto a parchment-lined baking sheet and cover with plastic wrap. Let the dough rise again for 30 to 40 minutes, or until they've risen just slightly.

9. Make the almond sugar while the dough has a second rise: In a small bowl, mix the sugar and almond extract to combine.

10. Preheat your air fryer to 375°F for 10 minutes. Using an oven mitt, carefully place the prepared parchment circle into the air fryer basket. Fry 3 donuts at a time on the parchment paper for 5 to 6 minutes. Rotate the donuts 180 degrees to ensure even frying, then fry for an additional 3 minutes, or until completely golden brown.

11. Place the donuts directly into the almond sugar and toss to coat. Set to cool completely on a cooling rack. Sprinkle the tops of each donut with the toasted, chopped almonds.

12. To fill the donuts: Once donuts have cooled, poke a hole into the top of each with a wooden skewer, twirling the skewer around to enlarge the hole slightly. Next, fill a large pastry bag with the apricot jam and cut the tip of the bag. Fit the tip of the pastry bag into the holes on top of the donuts and pipe about 1 to 2 tablespoons of jam inside.

Maple Bacon Glazed Donuts

I know the maple bacon donut is played out by now, but the air fryer maple bacon donut is not! Next time I would love to candy the bacon before adding it to these basically perfect donuts.

YIELD: 6   **PREP TIME:** 1 hour, 40 minutes   **COOK TIME:** 18 minutes

DONUTS:

½ cup whole milk, warmed to 110°F

½ tablespoon active dry yeast

2 tablespoons granulated sugar

1 large egg

3 tablespoons unsalted butter, melted and cooled

½ teaspoon vanilla extract

2 cups all-purpose flour, plus more for dusting and rolling

¼ teaspoon salt

3 strips bacon, cooked, drained, cooled, and chopped

GLAZE:

1 cup confectioners' sugar, sifted

3 to 3½ tablespoons maple syrup

2 tablespoons heavy cream

TO MAKE THE DONUTS:

1. Trace an 8-inch circle onto a piece of parchment paper. Cut out the circle and set aside.

2. Pour the warmed milk into the bowl of a stand mixer fitted with the dough hook attachment. Sprinkle in the yeast and ¼ teaspoon of the sugar on top of the milk. Stir with a spoon and let sit for 5 minutes or until the yeast has foamed and become frothy.

3. With the mixer set to low speed, add the remaining sugar, the egg, butter, vanilla, 1 cup of flour, and salt. Mix on low speed

for about 1 minute to combine. Add the remaining flour and mix on medium-high speed until the dough begins to pull away from the sides of the bowl. This dough will be thick and somewhat sticky.

4. With your hands, form the dough into a ball and turn out onto a lightly floured surface. Knead dough for 2 minutes and place into a greased bowl.

5. Cover the bowl with plastic wrap and let it rest and rise in a warm environment until doubled in size, 1 to 1½ hours.

6. Once properly rested and doubled in size, punch the dough down with your fist to release air bubbles. Turn out the dough onto a lightly floured surface. Roll the dough out to about ½ inch thick. Using a donut cutter, cut out 6 donuts.

7. Place the donuts on a small baking sheet lined with parchment paper. Cover with a kitchen towel and let rest for 10 minutes while you preheat your air fryer.

8. Preheat your air fryer to 375°F for 10 minutes.

9. Using an oven mitt, carefully place the prepared parchment circle into the air fryer basket. Place 2 donuts on the parchment and fry for 3 to 4 minutes, then rotate the donuts 180 degrees to ensure even frying. Fry for an additional 2 minutes, or until completely golden brown.

10. Make the glaze while the first batch is frying, and whisk all of the ingredients together in a medium bowl.

11. Remove the donuts from the air fryer and let cool on a cooling rack just slightly before glazing.

12. To glaze, dip each donut into the glaze, making sure to cover the top of each donut completely. Sprinkle the tops of each donut with the chopped bacon, and place back on the cooling rack to let the glaze dry. Repeat with the remaining donuts.

Strawberry Frosted Donuts

These donuts are covered with what is basically a strawberry buttercream. Shrug. Thick and sweet, the frosting makes these reminiscent of the famous donuts from *The Simpsons*. A fine donut to dunk into a big mug of the strongest Sunday morning coffee.

YIELD: 6   **PREP TIME:** 1 hour, 40 minutes   **COOK TIME:** 18 minutes

DONUTS:

½ cup whole milk, warmed to 110°F

½ tablespoon active dry yeast

2 tablespoons granulated sugar

1 large egg

3 tablespoons unsalted butter, melted and cooled

½ teaspoon vanilla extract

2 cups all-purpose flour, plus more for dusting and rolling

¼ teaspoon salt

sprinkles

FROSTING:

3 to 4 fresh strawberries

1 tablespoon strawberry jam

2 cups confectioners' sugar, sifted

TO MAKE THE DONUTS:

1. Trace an 8-inch circle onto a piece of parchment paper. Cut out the circle and set aside.

2. Pour the warmed milk into the bowl of a stand mixer fitted with the dough hook attachment. Sprinkle in the yeast and ¼ teaspoon of the sugar on top of the milk. Stir with a spoon and let sit for 5 minutes or until the yeast has foamed and become frothy.

3. With the mixer set to low speed, add the remaining sugar, the egg, butter, vanilla, 1 cup of flour, and salt. Mix on low speed for about 1 minute to combine. Add the remaining flour and mix on medium-high speed until the dough begins to pull away from the sides of the bowl. This dough will be thick and somewhat sticky.

4. With your hands, form dough into a ball and turn out onto a lightly floured surface. Knead dough for 2 minutes and place into a greased bowl.

5. Cover the bowl with plastic wrap and let it rest and rise in a warm environment until doubled in size, 1 to 1½ hours.

6. Once properly rested and doubled in size, punch the dough down with your fist to release air bubbles. Turn out the dough onto a lightly floured surface. Roll the dough out to about ½ inch thick. Using a donut cutter, cut out 6 donuts.

7. Place the donuts on a small baking sheet lined with parchment paper. Cover with a kitchen towel and let rest for 10 minutes while you preheat your air fryer.

8. Preheat your air fryer to 375°F for 10 minutes.

9. Using an oven mitt, carefully place the prepared parchment circle into the air fryer basket. Place 2 donuts on the parchment and fry for 3 to 4 minutes, then rotate the donuts 180 degrees to ensure even frying. Fry for an additional 2 minutes, or until completely golden brown.

10. Make the frosting while the first batch is frying: Slice the strawberries and puree in a food processor with the strawberry jam. Slowly pour in the confectioners' sugar, 1 cup at a time, until you've reached your desired consistency.

11. Remove the donuts from the air fryer and let cool on a cooling rack just slightly before glazing.

12. To frost, dunk each donut into the frosting, making sure to cover the top of each donut completely. Top with sprinkles, and place the donuts back on the cooling rack to let the frosting dry completely.

Classic Italian Zeppoles

An air fryer version of a deep-fried classic, and one of my new favorite desserts. A zeppole is Italian pastry rolled into balls and deep fried, donut-like. They are basically tiny donut holes that get rolled in sugar. You then devour them because zeppoles are delicious, and the air fryer version is no different.

YIELD: 10   **PREP TIME:** 1 hour, 40 minutes   **COOK TIME:** 25 minutes

½ cup warm water

½ teaspoon active dry yeast

½ tablespoon granulated sugar

½ teaspoon salt

1 cup all-purpose flour

½ tablespoon olive oil

confectioners' sugar, for dusting

TO MAKE THE ZEPPOLES:

1. Trace an 8-inch circle onto a piece of parchment paper. Cut out the circle and set aside.

2. In a small bowl, pour in the water, active dry yeast, granulated sugar, and salt. Stir to combine, and let the mixture stand until the yeast becomes foamy, about 5 minutes.

3. In a large bowl, combine the flour, yeast mixture, and olive oil. Stir with a wooden spoon until a sticky dough forms. Cover the bowl with plastic wrap and let the dough rise in a warm environment until doubled in size, about 1½ to 2 hours.

4. Once the dough has risen, preheat your air fryer to 370°F for 10 minutes. Using an oven mitt, carefully place the prepared parchment circle into the air fryer basket. Using two small spoons, scoop out some dough and shape into a round zeppole shape. Drop the zeppole into the air fryer basket on top of the parchment paper, and fill the air fryer basket with 2 or 3 more zeppole.

5. Fry the zeppole for 4 to 5 minutes, or until golden brown. Toss generously with confectioners' sugar and let cool on a cooking rack covered with paper towels. This dough will make about 10 zeppole, so frying in batches of 3 or 4 is a good idea.

Filled Zeppole

Here is a recipe for a filled zeppole, one in which I'm not telling you which kind of filling to use. Use whichever jam, jelly, or even chocolate hazelnut spread you'd like. The beauty is the simplicity. The beauty is the zeppole.

YIELD: 10   **PREP TIME:** 1 hour, 4 minutes   **COOK TIME:** 25 minutes

½ cup warm water

½ teaspoon active dry yeast

½ tablespoon granulated sugar

½ teaspoon salt

1 cup all-purpose flour

½ tablespoon olive oil

confectioners' sugar, for dusting

¼ to ½ cup jam, jelly, or chocolate hazelnut spread

TO MAKE THE ZEPPOLES:

1. Trace an 8-inch circle onto a piece of parchment paper. Cut out the circle and set aside.

2. In a small bowl, pour in the water, active dry yeast, granulated sugar, and salt. Stir to combine, and let the mixture stand until the yeast becomes foamy, about 5 minutes.

3. In a large bowl, combine the flour, yeast mixture, and olive oil. Stir with a wooden spoon until a sticky dough forms. Cover the bowl with plastic wrap and let the dough rise in a warm environment until doubled in size, about 1½ to 2 hours.

4. Once the dough has risen, preheat your air fryer to 370°F for 10 minutes. Using an oven mitt, carefully place the prepared parchment circle into the air fryer basket. Using two small spoons,

scoop out some dough and shape into a round zeppole shape. Drop the zeppole into the air fryer basket on top of the parchment paper, and fill the air fryer basket with 2 or 3 more zeppole.

5. Fry zeppole for 4 to 5 minutes, or until golden brown. Toss generously with confectioners' sugar and let cool on a cooking rack covered with paper towels.

6. Once cooled, poke a hole into the top of each zeppole with a wooden skewer and twirl the skewer to enlarge the hole slightly.

7. Fill a large piping bag with your filling of choice and cut off the tip of the bag. Insert the pastry bag tip into the hole on top of each zeppole, and pipe in about a tablespoon of filling. Serve immediately.

Classic Mexican Churros

My family frequented the flea market in our city when I was a kid. I loved going to see the vendors selling whatever various trinkets they were trying to get rid of. The flavors of my flea market were in the sweet batter of corn dogs, the crisp texture and pure saltiness of golden-brown french fries, and that beautiful, almost perfect burst of cinnamon sugar in the first bite of a churro, still hot from the deep fryer.

YIELD: 15   **PREP TIME:** 20 minutes   **COOK TIME:** 60 minutes

CHURROS:
½ cup water

½ tablespoon unsalted butter

½ tablespoon granulated sugar

¼ teaspoon vanilla extract

⅛ teaspoon salt

½ cup all-purpose flour

1 large egg

CINNAMON-SUGAR MIXTURE:
2 tablespoons unsalted butter, melted

¼ cup granulated sugar

¼ teaspoon ground cinnamon

TO MAKE THE CHURROS:

1. Trace an 8-inch circle onto a piece of parchment paper. Cut out the circle and set aside.

2. In a large saucepan set over medium heat, combine the water, butter, granulated sugar, vanilla extract, and salt, and bring to a boil.

3. Add all of the flour to the saucepan and with a wooden spoon, stir until no streaks of flour remain. Transfer the dough to the

bowl of a stand mixer fitted with the paddle attachment.

4. Mix the dough on medium-high speed until it has cooled slightly, 1 to 2 minutes. Reduce the speed to low, add the egg, and mix until incorporated. Increase the speed to high and mix until the dough has cooled completely, about 12 minutes.

5. Preheat your air fryer to 350°F for 10 minutes.

6. Transfer the dough to a pastry bag with a closed star tip. Using an oven mitt, carefully place the prepared parchment circle into the air fryer basket. Pipe 3-inch-long churros on top of the parchment circle in the air fryer basket, using scissors to snip the ends. In a 3-quart air fryer, I was able to fry churros in batches of 4.

7. Fry churros for 15 minutes, or until golden brown.

8. While the churros fry, make the cinnamon-sugar mixture: In a small bowl, pour the melted butter. In a separate small bowl, stir the granulated sugar and cinnamon to combine.

9. Remove the churros from the air fryer and dunk into the melted butter, then into the cinnamon-sugar. Set churros on a cooling rack covered with paper towels and let cool slightly before serving. Repeat with the remaining churro dough.

Brown Butter Donuts

Here we are using my favorite ingredient, brown butter, again. These donuts are slightly sweet, slightly savory, and totally delicious.

YIELD: 6   **PREP TIME:** 1 hour, 40 minutes   **COOK TIME:** 18 minutes

½ cup whole milk, warmed to 110°F

½ tablespoon active dry yeast

2 tablespoons granulated sugar, divided

1 large egg

3½ tablespoons unsalted butter, browned and cooled (page 10)

½ teaspoon almond extract

2 cups all-purpose flour, plus more for dusting and rolling

¼ teaspoon salt

confectioners' sugar, for dusting

TO MAKE THE DONUTS:

1. Trace an 8-inch circle onto a piece of parchment paper. Cut out the circle and set aside.

2. Pour the warmed milk into the bowl of a stand mixer fitted with the dough hook attachment. Sprinkle in the yeast and ¼ teaspoon of the sugar on top of the milk. Stir with a spoon and let sit for 5 minutes or until the yeast has foamed and become frothy.

3. With the mixer set to low speed, add the remaining sugar, the egg, browned butter, almond extract, 1 cup of the flour, and the salt. Mix on low speed for about 1 minute to combine. Add the remaining flour and mix on medium-high speed until the dough begins to pull away from the sides of the bowl. This dough will be thick and somewhat sticky.

4. With your hands, form the dough into a ball and turn out onto a lightly floured surface. Knead the dough for 2 minutes and place into a greased bowl.

5. Cover the bowl with plastic wrap and let it rest and rise in a warm environment until doubled in size, 1 to 1½ hours.

6. Once properly rested and doubled in size, punch the dough down with your fist to release air bubbles. Turn out the dough onto a lightly floured surface. Roll the dough out to about ½ inch thick. Using a donut cutter, cut out 6 donuts.

7. Place the donuts on a small baking sheet lined with parchment paper. Cover with a kitchen towel and let rest for 10 minutes while you preheat your air fryer.

8. Preheat your air fryer to 375°F for 10 minutes.

9. Using an oven mitt, carefully place the prepared parchment circle into the air fryer basket.

Place 2 donuts inside the air fryer basket and fry for 3 to 4 minutes, and then rotate the donuts 180 degrees to ensure even frying. Fry for an additional 2 minutes, or until completely golden brown.

10. Remove the donuts from air fryer and immediately dust with confectioners' sugar. Serve warm. Repeat with the remaining donuts.

Apple Cider Donuts

I adapted these beautiful apple cider donuts from the food section of the *New York Times* website. Apple cider is such an autumn-forward flavor, but I find myself craving these donuts year round. This is another cake-based donut, rather than a yeast donut.

YIELD: 1 dozen   **PREP TIME:** 50 minutes   **COOK TIME:** 24 minutes

1¼ cups granulated sugar, divided

1¾ teaspoons ground cinnamon, divided

½ cup apple cider

2¾ cups all-purpose flour

¾ teaspoons baking powder

½ teaspoon baking soda

⅛ teaspoon salt

⅛ teaspoon ground nutmeg

2 tablespoons unsalted butter, at room temperature

2 tablespoons packed light brown sugar

1 large egg, at room temperature

½ teaspoon vanilla extract

¼ cup buttermilk

½ medium Honeycrisp apple, diced

TO MAKE THE DONUTS:

1. Trace an 8-inch circle onto a piece of parchment paper. Cut the circle out and set aside.

2. In a small bowl, stir together ½ cup of the granulated sugar and 1 teaspoon of the cinnamon to combine. Set aside.

3. In a small saucepan over high heat, reduce the apple cider to about ¼ cup. Remove from the heat and set aside to cool.

4. In a large bowl, whisk together the flour, baking powder, baking soda, salt, nutmeg, and remaining ¾ teaspoon cinnamon to combine.

5. In the bowl of a stand mixer fitted with the paddle attachment, combine the butter, brown sugar, and remaining ¾ cup granulated sugar, and mix on medium speed to combine. Add the egg and mix well, scraping down the sides of the bowl as needed. Mix in the vanilla extract, buttermilk, and the reduced apple cider.

6. Add the dry ingredients to the wet ingredients and mix well to combine. Fold in the diced apples by hand and cover the bowl with plastic wrap. Refrigerate for 30 minutes.

7. Preheat your air fryer to 375°F for 10 minutes.

8. Turn the dough out onto a lightly floured surface, and roll out into a ½-inch-thick rough disk. Cut out 12 donuts using a 2½-inch donut cutter.

9. Using an oven mitt, carefully place the prepared parchment circle into the air fryer basket.

Place 3 donuts on the parchment and fry for 3 to 4 minutes. Rotate the donuts 180 degrees to ensure even browning, and fry for an additional 2 minutes, or until completely golden brown.

10. Sprinkle the prepared cinnamon-sugar mixture over the donuts and serve warm. Repeat with the remaining donuts.

Cereal Donuts

Use your favorite breakfast cereal, or a combination of flavors. My favorites are fruity cereals, overly sugary corn-based cereal, and of course any chocolate-flavored cereal is all right with me. These would be good donuts to let your kids decorate.

YIELD: 6 **PREP TIME:** 1 hour, 40 minutes **COOK TIME:** 18 minutes

DONUTS:
1 cup breakfast cereal

½ cup whole milk, warmed to 110°F

½ tablespoon active dry yeast

2 tablespoons granulated sugar, divided

1 large egg

3 tablespoons unsalted butter, melted and cooled

½ teaspoon vanilla extract

2 cups all-purpose flour, plus more for dusting and rolling

¼ teaspoon salt

GLAZE:
1 cup confectioners' sugar, sifted

2 tablespoons plus 2 teaspoons heavy cream

¼ teaspoon vanilla extract

TO MAKE THE DONUTS:

1. Trace an 8-inch circle onto a piece of parchment paper. Cut out the circle and set aside.

2. Pour the breakfast cereal into a large bowl and set aside.

3. Pour the warmed milk into the bowl of a stand mixer fitted with the dough hook attachment. Sprinkle in the yeast and ¼ teaspoon of the sugar on top of the milk. Stir with a spoon and let sit for 5 minutes or until the yeast has foamed and become frothy.

4. With the mixer set to low speed, add the remaining sugar, the egg, butter, vanilla, 1 cup of the flour, and the salt. Mix on low speed for about 1 minute to combine. Add the remaining flour and mix on medium-high speed until the dough begins to pull away from the sides of the bowl. This dough will be thick and somewhat sticky.

5. With your hands, form the dough into a ball and turn out onto a lightly floured surface. Knead the dough for 2 minutes and place into a greased bowl.

6. Cover the bowl with plastic wrap and let it rest and rise in a warm environment until doubled in size, 1 to 1½ hours.

7. Once properly rested and doubled in size, punch the dough down with your fist to release air bubbles. Turn out the dough onto a lightly floured surface. Roll the dough out to about ½ inch thick. Using a donut cutter, cut out 6 donuts.

8. Place the donuts on a small baking sheet lined with parchment paper. Cover with a kitchen towel and let rest for 10 minutes while you preheat your air fryer.

9. Preheat your air fryer to 375°F for 10 minutes.

10. Using an oven mitt, carefully place the prepared parchment circle into the air fryer basket. Place 2 donuts onto the parchment and fry for 3 to 4 minutes, then rotate the donuts 180 degrees to ensure even frying. Fry for an additional 2 minutes, or until completely golden brown.

11. Make the glaze while the first batch is frying: Whisk all of the ingredients in a medium bowl to combine.

12. Remove donuts from air fryer and let cool on a cooling rack just slightly before glazing.

13. To glaze, dip each donut into the glaze, making sure to cover the tops of the donuts. Immediately dunk the glazed donuts into the cereal. Place back on the cooling rack to let the glaze dry. Repeat with the remaining donuts.

Blueberry Glazed Donuts

A tart glaze for a yeasty donut is a classic, and now the air fryer version is too.

YIELD: 6   **PREP TIME:** 1 hour, 40 minutes   **COOK TIME:** 18 minutes

DONUTS:

½ cup whole milk, warmed to 110°F

½ tablespoon active dry yeast

2 tablespoons granulated sugar, divided

1 large egg

3 tablespoons unsalted butter, melted and cooled

½ teaspoon vanilla extract

2 cups all-purpose flour, plus more for dusting and rolling

¼ teaspoon salt

BLUEBERRY GLAZE:

¼ cup fresh blueberries

½ tablespoon freshly squeezed lemon juice

1 cup confectioners' sugar, sifted

2 tablespoons plus 2 teaspoons heavy cream

¼ teaspoon vanilla extract

TO MAKE THE DONUTS:

1. Trace an 8-inch circle onto a piece of parchment paper. Cut out the circle and set aside.

2. Pour the warmed milk into the bowl of a stand mixer fitted with the dough hook attachment. Sprinkle in the yeast and ¼ teaspoon of the sugar on top of the milk. Stir with a spoon and let sit for 5 minutes or until the yeast has foamed and become frothy.

3. With the mixer set to low speed, add the remaining sugar, the egg, butter, vanilla, 1 cup of flour, and salt. Mix on low speed for about 1 minute to combine. Add the remaining flour and mix on medium-high speed until the dough begins to pull away from the sides of the bowl. This dough will be thick and somewhat sticky.

4. With your hands, form dough into a ball and turn out onto a lightly floured surface. Knead dough for 2 minutes and place into a greased bowl.

5. Cover the bowl with plastic wrap and let it rest and rise in a warm environment until doubled in size, 1 to 1½ hours.

6. Once properly rested and doubled in size, punch the dough down with your fist to release air bubbles. Turn out the dough onto a lightly floured surface. Roll the dough out to about ½ inch thick. Using a donut cutter, cut out 6 donuts.

7. Place the donuts on a small baking sheet lined with parchment paper. Cover with a kitchen towel and let rest for 10 minutes while you preheat your air fryer.

8. Preheat your air fryer to 375°F for 10 minutes.

9. Using an oven mitt, carefully place the prepared parchment circle into the air fryer basket. Place 2 donuts on the parchment and fry for 3 to 4 minutes, then rotate the donuts 180 degrees to ensure even frying. Fry for an additional 2 minutes, or until completely golden brown.

10. Make the glaze while the first batch is frying: In a small saucepan, heat the blueberries and lemon juice until the blueberries begin to release their juices. Remove from the heat and let cool slightly before pureeing the mixture in a food processor. Pour the puree into a medium bowl, and whisk in the confectioners' sugar, heavy cream, and vanilla extract to combine.

11. Remove the donuts from the air fryer and let cool on a cooling rack just slightly before glazing.

12. To glaze, dip each donut into the glaze, making sure to cover the tops of the donuts. Place back on the cooling rack to let the glaze dry. Repeat with the remaining donuts.

Vanilla Bean Glazed Donut

Vanilla bean seeds in the glaze makes this a donut for any vanilla lover.

YIELD: 6   **PREP TIME:** 1 hour, 40 minutes   **COOK TIME:** 18 minutes

DONUTS:

½ cup whole milk, warmed
to 110°F

½ tablespoon active dry yeast

2 tablespoons granulated sugar,
divided

1 large egg

3 tablespoons unsalted butter,
melted and cooled

½ teaspoon vanilla extract

2 cups all-purpose flour,
plus more for dusting and rolling

¼ teaspoon salt

GLAZE:

1 cup confectioners' sugar, sifted

2 tablespoons plus 2 teaspoons
heavy cream

½ vanilla bean, seeds scraped

TO MAKE THE DONUTS:

1. Trace an 8-inch circle onto a piece of parchment paper. Cut out the circle and set aside.

2. Pour the warmed milk into the bowl of a stand mixer fitted with the dough hook attachment. Sprinkle in the yeast and ¼ teaspoon of the sugar on top of the milk. Stir with a spoon and let sit for 5 minutes or until the yeast has foamed and become frothy.

3. With the mixer set to low speed, add the remaining sugar, the egg, butter, vanilla, 1 cup of flour, and salt. Mix on low speed for about 1 minute to combine. Add the remaining flour and mix on medium-high speed until the dough begins to pull away from the

sides of the bowl. This dough will be thick and somewhat sticky.

4. With your hands, form dough into a ball and turn out onto a lightly floured surface. Knead dough for 2 minutes and place into a greased bowl.

5. Cover the bowl with plastic wrap and let it rest and rise in a warm environment until doubled in size, 1 to 1½ hours.

6. Once properly rested and doubled in size, punch the dough down with your fist to release air bubbles. Turn out the dough onto a lightly floured surface. Roll the dough out to about ½ inch thick. Using a donut cutter, cut out 6 donuts.

7. Place the donuts on a small baking sheet lined with parchment paper. Cover with a kitchen towel and let rest for 10 minutes while you preheat your air fryer.

8. Preheat your air fryer to 375°F for 10 minutes.

9. Using an oven mitt, carefully place the prepared parchment circle into the air fryer basket. Place 2 donuts on the parchment and fry for 3 to 4 minutes, then rotate the donuts 180 degrees to ensure even frying. Fry for an additional 2 minutes, or until completely golden brown.

10. Make the glaze while the first batch is frying: Whisk all the ingredients together in a medium bowl.

11. Remove the donuts from the air fryer and let cool on a cooling rack just slightly before glazing.

12. To glaze, dip each donut into the glaze, making sure to cover the tops of the donuts. Place back on the cooling rack to let the glaze dry. Repeat with the remaining donuts.

QUICK BREADS, BISCUITS, AND BREAD PUDDINGS

There is an abundance of air fryer bread pudding recipes in this chapter. There is also banana bread with chocolate chips and sweet buttermilk biscuits, but the majority of the goods we will be working with for dessert breads are bread puddings. You will want to order a set of 5 x 3 x 2-inch loaf pans, as these will be mini breads and loaves. These sweet breads won't need time to rise since we aren't using yeast, as we did for donuts.

Bread pudding is such a decadent, indulgent dessert, even in miniature form. I used mostly brioche for these recipes, but they can easily be adapted for other kinds of breads like croissants, cinnamon bread, and even sourdough. The possibilities are plentiful when it comes to flavoring your custard for bread pudding. You could spike the milk for the custard base with vanilla bean seeds in lieu of vanilla extract; try adding a tablespoon of amaretto for an almond flavor, or orange zest if you want to bring out some citrus notes in your bread pudding.

Banana Chocolate Chip Bread

The very first thing I ever baked on my own was a banana bread that I had to make for homework for my sixth-grade home economics class. I remember the feeling of total satisfaction and pride in myself that I had managed to re-create the flavor and look of the banana bread we'd had in class that day. Adding chocolate chips to this air fryer version seemed like a great idea, something 12-year-old Teresa would definitely appreciate.

YIELD: three 5 x 3 x 2-inch loaf cakes **PREP TIME:** 15 minutes
COOK TIME: 90 minutes

¾ *cup granulated sugar*

½ *cup (1 stick) unsalted butter, at room temperature*

2 large eggs, at room temperature

2 medium bananas, mashed

½ *teaspoon vanilla extract*

1½ *cups all-purpose flour*

1 cup semisweet chocolate chips

½ *teaspoon baking soda*

½ *teaspoon salt*

TO MAKE THE BANANA BREAD:

1. Grease three 5 x 3 x 2-inch loaf pans with cooking spray.

2. In the bowl of a stand mixer fitted with the paddle attachment, cream the butter and sugar on medium-high speed until light and fluffy, 1 to 2 minutes. Add the eggs, one at a time, and continue mixing to incorporate.

3. Add the bananas and vanilla extract and mix on low speed until combined.

4. Preheat your air fryer to 350°F for 10 minutes.

5. Incorporate the flour, chocolate chips, baking soda, and salt into the batter and mix well. Spoon the batter into the prepared loaf pans and bake one at a time for 25 to 30 minutes each, or until a toothpick inserted into the bread comes out clean. Let cool slightly before serving.

Buttermilk Cinnamon Biscuits

The addition of cinnamon in these biscuits is divine, making them a sweet, dessert biscuit. Serve with ice cream to really be the talk of the air fryer desserts town.

YIELD: 10 mini biscuits   **PREP TIME:** 15 minutes   **COOK TIME:** 24 minutes

1¼ cups all-purpose flour, plus more for dusting

½ cup cake flour

½ teaspoon baking powder

¼ teaspoon baking soda

1 teaspoon granulated sugar

1 teaspoon ground cinnamon

¾ teaspoon salt

4 tablespoons cold unsalted butter, cut into cubes

¾ cup buttermilk

3 tablespoons unsalted butter, melted

TO MAKE THE BISCUITS:

1. Trace an 8-inch circle onto a piece of parchment paper. Cut out the circle and set aside.

2. In a medium bowl, whisk together the all-purpose flour, cake flour, baking powder, baking soda, granulated sugar, cinnamon, and salt to combine. Using a pastry cutter or your fingers, cut the cold butter into the flour. Toss the butter with the flour to coat, working quickly and confidently.

3. Pour the buttermilk into the flour-butter mixture and stir with a rubber spatula until a dough forms. Turn the biscuit dough out onto a lightly floured surface. Pat the dough out with your hands into a disk about 8 inches across and ½ inch thick.

4. Using a 1½-inch round cutter, cut out 10 biscuits, making sure to press straight down with the cutter.

5. Preheat your air fryer to 400°F for 10 minutes. Using an oven mitt, carefully place the prepared parchment circle into the air fryer basket. Place 4 biscuits on top of the parchment circle and bake for 8 minutes, or until the biscuits have browned slightly.

6. Brush the biscuits with melted butter and serve immediately.

Classic Bread Pudding

I am the biggest bread pudding fan after making this classic recipe. In the air fryer the custard becomes luscious, while the edges of the brioche crisp slightly.

YIELD: 3 servings **PREP TIME:** 20 minutes **COOK TIME:** 40 minutes

1 cup whole milk

1 tablespoon unsalted butter

½ teaspoon vanilla extract

2 tablespoons plus 2 teaspoons granulated sugar

pinch of salt

1½ cups cubed brioche, cut into 1-inch pieces

1 large egg, beaten

whipped cream, for topping (optional)

TO MAKE THE BREAD PUDDING:

1. Grease a 6 x 2-inch round cake pan with cooking spray.

2. Preheat your air fryer to 250°F for 15 minutes.

3. In a small saucepan over medium heat, whisk together the milk, butter, vanilla, granulated sugar, and salt to combine. Continue cooking until the butter has melted. Remove from the heat and let cool.

4. Fill the prepared cake pan with cubed brioche. Add the egg to the cooled milk mixture and whisk to incorporate. Pour the mixture over the bread and bake in your air fryer for 35 to 40 minutes, or until the custard is set and the bread has browned slightly. Serve warm and top with whipped cream, if desired.

Golden Raisin Bread Pudding

Golden raisins are such beautiful ingredients, I knew I wanted to use them for this book. Featured alongside a luscious custard, the raisins elevate classic bread pudding.

YIELD: 2 to 3 servings   **PREP TIME:** 25 minutes   **COOK TIME:** 40 minutes

1½ cups cubed brioche, cut into 1-inch pieces

1 large egg

⅔ cup whole milk

3 tablespoons packed light brown sugar

1½ tablespoons brown butter, cooled (page 10)

½ teaspoon ground ginger

¼ teaspoon ground cinnamon

dash of salt

⅓ cup golden raisins

TO MAKE THE BREAD PUDDING:

1. Grease a 6 x 2-inch round cake pan with cooking spray.

2. Place the cubed brioche into the prepared cake pan. In a medium bowl, whisk the egg, milk, brown sugar, cooled brown butter, ginger, cinnamon, and salt to combine. Stir the raisins into mixture and pour over the brioche. Let the bread pudding stand for 15 minutes while you preheat your air fryer to 250°F.

3. Bake in your air fryer for 35 to 40 minutes, or until toothpick inserted in the center comes out clean.

Milk Chocolate Croissant Bread Pudding

This is basically chocolate milk–soaked croissants, and that is as tasty as it sounds.

YIELD: 3 servings   **PREP TIME:** 30 minutes   **COOK TIME:** 35 minutes

1 cup whole milk

⅓ vanilla bean, seeds scraped

⅛ teaspoon salt

3 ounces milk chocolate, roughly chopped, divided

2 large eggs

2 large croissants, cut into 1-inch cubes

TO MAKE BREAD PUDDING:

1. Grease a 6 x 2-inch round cake pan with cooking spray.

2. Preheat your air fryer to 250°F for 15 minutes.

3. In a medium saucepan over medium-low heat, bring the milk, vanilla bean seeds, and salt to a simmer. Cover and let stand, off the heat, for 10 minutes. Add half of the chopped chocolate to the warm milk and whisk to combine. Let the milk chocolate mixture cool for an additional 15 minutes.

4. Whisk in the eggs and set aside.

5. Add the croissant pieces to the prepared cake pan with the remaining chopped chocolate and stir to combine. Pour the chocolate milk over the croissant pieces and bake in your air fryer for 35 minutes, or until the custard has set and the edges of the croissant pieces have crisped slightly. Serve warm.

Pumpkin Chocolate Chip Bread

Definitely make these for a Halloween party. Guests will love the flavor combination of pumpkin and chocolate, and these breads will of course fit the orange and black theme.

YIELD: two 5 x 3 x 2-inch bread loaves **PREP TIME:** 15 minutes
COOK TIME: 50 minutes

1¾ cups all-purpose flour

1½ teaspoons pumpkin pie spice

1 teaspoon baking soda

½ teaspoon baking powder

½ teaspoon salt

½ cup granulated sugar

½ cup vegetable oil

2 large eggs, at room temperature

½ (15-ounce) can pureed pumpkin

¼ cup water

1 cup semisweet chocolate chips

TO MAKE THE BREAD:

1. Preheat your air fryer to 350°F for 10 minutes. Grease two 5 x 3 x 2-inch loaf pans with cooking spray.

2. In a large bowl, whisk together the flour, pumpkin pie spice, baking soda, baking powder, and salt to combine. In a medium bowl, whisk together the sugar, oil, eggs, pureed pumpkin, and water to combine. Add the wet ingredients to the dry ingredients, and stir to combine well. Fold in the chocolate chips and divide the batter evenly between the prepared loaf pans.

3. Bake the loaves in the air fryer one at a time for 20 to 25 minutes each, or until a toothpick inserted into the center of the bread comes out mostly free of crumbs. Cool completely before serving.

Lemon Glazed Loaf

Lemon adds a nice tartness to this loaf. The yield is a whopping one miniature loaf bread, making this a perfect dessert for one or two people.

YIELD: one 5 x 3 x 2-inch loaf   **PREP TIME:** 10 minutes   **COOK TIME:** 25 minutes

½ cup all-purpose flour

¼ teaspoon baking powder

¼ teaspoon salt

3 tablespoons unsalted butter, melted

⅓ cup granulated sugar

1 large egg, at room temperature

2 tablespoons full-fat sour cream, at room temperature

1 teaspoon lemon zest (from about 1 small lemon)

¼ teaspoon almond extract

½ cup confectioners' sugar

1 tablespoon freshly squeezed lemon juice

TO MAKE THE LOAF:

1. Grease a 5 x 3 x 2-inch loaf pan with cooking spray. Preheat your air fryer to 350°F for 10 minutes.

2. In a small bowl, whisk together the flour, baking powder, and salt to combine.

3. In a medium bowl, whisk together the melted butter, granulated sugar, egg, sour cream, lemon zest, and almond extract to fully incorporate. Gently fold in the flour mixture and stir just to combine.

4. Pour the batter into prepared loaf pan and bake in the air fryer for 13 to 15 minutes, or until a toothpick inserted in the center comes out clean. Set on a cooling rack slightly.

5. Make the glaze while the loaf cools: In a small bowl, whisk the confectioners' sugar and lemon juice to combine. Drizzle the glaze over the warm loaf and serve immediately.

Lemon Blueberry Bread Pudding

This recipe uses some of the most summery flavors I could think of: lemon and blueberry. Feel free to switch up the type of bread. I'm using brioche here, but this would work well with croissants and even a day-old cinnamon bread.

YIELD: 4 servings   **PREP TIME:** 35 minutes   **COOK TIME:** 45 minutes

1 large egg

½ cup heavy cream

½ cup whole milk

¼ cup packed light brown sugar

¼ teaspoon almond extract

½ teaspoon lemon zest (from ½ small lemon)

1½ cups cubed brioche, cut into 1-inch pieces

¼ cup fresh blueberries

1 tablespoon unsalted butter, melted

TO MAKE THE BREAD PUDDING:

1. Grease a 6 x 2-inch round cake pan with cooking spray.

2. In a large bowl, whisk together the egg, heavy cream, milk, light brown sugar, almond extract, and lemon zest to combine. Add the brioche and the fresh blueberries to the mixture and toss to coat. Mix in the melted butter and let sit for 30 minutes.

3. Preheat your air fryer to 250°F for 10 minutes.

4. Pour the bread mixture into the prepared cake pan and bake in your air fryer for 35 to 40 minutes, or until the middle has set. Serve warm.

Chocolate Bread Pudding

Chocolate bread pudding is one of those things that sounds too decadent until you bite into it. Then you realize it's extremely decadent—and it's your new favorite dessert. I'd drizzle a caramel sauce on this before serving.

YIELD: 3 servings   **PREP TIME:** 30 minutes   **COOK TIME:** 40 minutes

3 ounces milk chocolate, chopped

6 tablespoons whole milk

¼ cup heavy cream

1 large egg

1 large egg yolk

2½ tablespoons granulated sugar, divided

¼ teaspoon vanilla extract

⅛ teaspoon salt

2½ cups cubed brioche, cut into 1-inch pieces

TO MAKE THE BREAD PUDDING:

1. Grease a 6 x 2-inch round cake pan with cooking spray.

2. Place the chopped chocolate in a heatproof bowl and set over a small pot of simmering water. Stir the chocolate with a rubber spatula until the chocolate has melted. Remove from the heat and let cool.

3. In a medium saucepan over medium heat, bring the milk and cream to a simmer. In a large bowl, whisk together the egg, egg yolk, 2 tablespoons of the granulated sugar, and the vanilla extract and salt to combine. Slowly whisk the hot milk mixture into the bowl, then the cooled melted chocolate. Stir to combine.

4. Place the brioche cubes into the prepared cake pan and pour the chocolate mixture over the brioche. Let stand for 20 minutes.

5. Preheat your air fryer to 250°F for 10 minutes. Sprinkle the remaining granulated sugar on top of the bread pudding and bake in your air fryer for 35 to 40 minutes, or until the custard has set and the edges of the brioche have crisped slightly. Serve warm.

Pumpkin Spice Bread Pudding

The most basic of autumn flavors, which I love no matter how basic that is.

YIELD: 4 servings   **PREP TIME:** 15 minutes   **COOK TIME:** 45 minutes

½ (15-ounce) can pureed pumpkin

6 tablespoons granulated sugar

1 teaspoon pumpkin pie spice

1 large egg

½ cup whole milk

2 tablespoons half-and-half

½ teaspoon vanilla extract

2½ cups cubed brioche, cut into 1-inch pieces

TO MAKE THE BREAD PUDDING:

1. Grease a 6 x 2-inch round cake pan with cooking spray.

2. Preheat your air fryer to 250°F for 10 minutes

3. In a large bowl, whisk the pureed pumpkin, granulated sugar, and pumpkin pie spice to combine. Add the egg and continue whisking. Gradually whisk in the milk, half-and-half, and vanilla extract. Toss in the cubed brioche and stir to coat. Let stand for 10 minutes.

4. Pour the bread mixture into the prepared cake pan and bake in your air fryer for 45 minutes, or until the custard has set and the edges of the brioche have crisped slightly. Serve warm.

Bread Pudding with Warm Bourbon Sauce

Feel free to omit the bourbon from the sauce, but if you're a fan of the spirit, this bread pudding is for you. Use a bourbon you'd be happy to drink straight from the bottle, as the flavor will be highlighted in the sauce.

YIELD: 2 servings   **PREP TIME:** 1 hour, 10 minutes (includes chilling)
COOK TIME: 40 minutes

BREAD PUDDING:
2 large eggs

½ cup whole milk

½ cup heavy cream

2 tablespoons granulated sugar

½ teaspoon vanilla extract

pinch of salt

2 cups cubed day-old brioche, cut into ½-inch pieces

¼ cup pecans, toasted and chopped

BOURBON SAUCE:
2 tablespoons unsalted butter

¼ cup granulated sugar

1½ tablespoons heavy cream

1 tablespoon bourbon

TO MAKE THE BREAD PUDDING:

1. Grease a 6 x 2-inch round cake pan with cooking spray.

2. In a medium bowl, whisk together the eggs, milk, heavy cream, granulated sugar, vanilla extract, and salt to combine. Place the brioche and the pecans into the prepared cake pan.

3. Pour the custard mixture over the bread and pecans, and push down to fully submerge. Refrigerate for 1 hour.

4. Preheat your air fryer to 250°F for 10 minutes. Bake the bread

pudding in the air fryer for 40 minutes, or until the custard has set and the edges of the brioche have crisped slightly.

5. While the bread pudding is baking, make the bourbon sauce: In a small saucepan set over medium heat, melt the butter. Whisk in the granulated sugar, heavy cream, and bourbon. Simmer the mixture until thickened, about 2 minutes.

6. Spoon the bourbon sauce over the bread pudding. Serve warm.

Coconut Bread Pudding

The aroma of this coconut custard is very tropical and lovely. I'd pair this bread pudding with a mango coulis, or even a side of mango ice cream.

YIELD: 4 servings   **PREP TIME:** 20 minutes   **COOK TIME:** 45 minutes

2 large eggs

6 tablespoons granulated sugar

½ (13.5-ounce) can coconut milk

1 cup whole milk

¼ teaspoon ground cinnamon

½ teaspoon vanilla extract

pinch of salt

3½ cups cubed brioche, cut into ½-inch pieces

confectioners' sugar, for dusting (optional)

TO MAKE THE BREAD PUDDING:

1. Grease a 6 x 2-inch round cake pan with cooking spray.

2. Preheat your air fryer to 250°F for 10 minutes.

3. In a large bowl, whisk the eggs, granulated sugar, coconut milk, whole milk, ground cinnamon, vanilla extract, and salt to combine. Add the brioche and toss to coat, pushing down on the mixture to fully submerge. Let stand on your counter for 5 minutes.

4. Pour the bread pudding into the prepared cake pan and bake in the air fryer for 45 minutes, or until the custard has set and the edges of the brioche have crisped slightly. Dust with confectioners' sugar, if desired, and serve warm.

Pear and Chocolate Brioche Pudding

The sweetness of the pear works well with the slightly bitter chocolate, making this my favorite of the air fryer bread puddings.

YIELD: 4 servings   **PREP TIME:** 10 minutes   **COOK TIME:** 40 minutes

2 ounces bittersweet chocolate, roughly chopped

3 cups cubed brioche, cut into ½-inch pieces

1 Bartlett pear, cored and thinly sliced

1 large egg

1 large egg yolk

¾ cup whole milk

⅔ cup heavy cream

¼ cup packed light brown sugar

½ teaspoon ground cinnamon

pinch of salt

TO MAKE THE BRIOCHE PUDDING:

1. Grease a 6 x 2-inch round cake pan with cooking spray. Sprinkle the bottom of the pan with the chopped chocolate and set aside.

2. Preheat your air fryer to 250°F for 10 minutes.

3. Place the brioche and sliced pears in the prepared cake pan and gently toss to combine with the chopped chocolate.

4. In a large bowl, whisk together the egg, egg yolk, milk, heavy cream, brown sugar, cinnamon, and salt to combine. Pour the custard over the brioche and pear mixture, and let stand on your counter for 5 minutes.

5. Bake the bread pudding in the air fryer for 40 minutes, or until the custard has set and the edges of the brioche have crisped slightly. Serve warm.

Croissant Pudding

Croissant lovers will be pleased with this air fryer croissant pudding, but so will anyone who appreciates a simple but delicious dessert.

YIELD: 2 servings   **PREP TIME:** 15 minutes   **COOK TIME:** 40 minutes

1 large egg

⅓ cup granulated sugar

1 cup whole milk

pinch of salt

2 croissants, torn into large pieces

1½ tablespoons slivered almonds, toasted

TO MAKE THE BREAD PUDDING:

1. Grease a 6 x 2-inch round cake pan with cooking spray.

2. In a large bowl, whisk together the egg, granulated sugar, milk, and salt to combine. Add the croissant pieces to the bowl and stir to coat. Let the bread pudding stand on your counter for 10 minutes while you preheat your air fryer to 250°F.

3. Transfer the mixture to the prepared cake pan, sprinkle with slivered, toasted almonds, and bake in your air fryer for 35 to 40 minutes, until the custard has set and the edges of the croissant pieces have crisped slightly. Serve warm.

Orange Chocolate Bread Pudding

The orange and chocolate flavor pairing reminds me of a certain orange and chocolate candy my grandparents sometimes had around at Christmas. The bright citrus and bittersweet chocolate in this bread pudding makes it one to serve year-round, though.

YIELD: 3 servings   **PREP TIME:** 15 minutes   **COOK TIME:** 40 minutes

1 cup whole milk

¼ cup granulated sugar

2 ounces bittersweet chocolate, roughly chopped

2 large eggs, beaten lightly

½ tablespoon orange zest (from about 1 small orange)

¼ teaspoon vanilla extract

⅛ teaspoon salt

whipped cream, optional

TO MAKE THE BREAD PUDDING:

1. Grease a 6 x 2-inch round cake pan with cooking spray. Spread French bread cubes into prepared cake pan and set aside.

2. Preheat your air fryer to 250°F for 15 minutes.

3. In a small saucepan set over medium heat, combine the milk, granulated sugar, and roughly chopped chocolate. Whisk mixture frequently until chocolate has melted. Remove from heat.

4. In a medium bowl, add the eggs, orange zest, vanilla extract, and salt, and whisk just until combined. Slowly whisk in the chocolate mixture, then pour the custard over the French bread cubes in the prepared cake pan.

5. Bake bread pudding in the air fryer for 35 to 40 minutes, or until the custard has set and the edges of the French bread have crisped slightly. Serve warm and top with whipped cream, if desired.

Cinnamon-Raisin Bread Pudding

My mom used to make cinnamon-raisin toast for us growing up, and this reminds me of that. I am glad I was able to re-create some of my earliest food memories via the air fryer; this bread pudding is symbolic of that.

YIELD: 2 servings   **PREP TIME:** 35 minutes   **COOK TIME:** 40 minutes

2 large eggs

1 ¼ cups milk

2 tablespoons plus 2 teaspoons packed light brown sugar

½ teaspoon salt

1 ½ tablespoons unsalted butter, melted

½ teaspoon ground cinnamon

¼ teaspoon ground nutmeg

1 ½ cups cubed cinnamon-raisin bread, cut into ½-inch pieces

TO MAKE THE BREAD PUDDING:

1. Grease a 6 x 2-inch round cake pan with cooking spray.

2. In a medium bowl, whisk together the eggs, milk, brown sugar, salt, melted butter, cinnamon, and nutmeg. Add the cinnamon-raisin bread to the prepared cake pan and pour the custard over. Let stand on your counter for 30 minutes.

3. Preheat your air fryer to 250°F for 10 minutes.

4. Bake the bread pudding in the air fryer for 35 to 40 minutes, or until the custard has set and the edges of the cinnamon bread have crisped slightly. Serve warm.

Small-Batch Cinnamon Rolls

These are for when you want cinnamon rolls but don't want to be in the kitchen all morning. I used frozen bread dough, which I found randomly one day while at Target. Make these for a relaxed Sunday morning.

YIELD: 4   **PREP TIME:** 1 hour, 40 minutes   **COOK TIME:** 10 minutes

CINNAMON ROLLS:

½ pound frozen bread dough, thawed

2 tablespoons unsalted butter, melted

6 tablespoons packed light brown sugar

½ tablespoon ground cinnamon

ORANGE CREAM CHEESE GLAZE:

2 ounces cream cheese, at room temperature

1 tablespoon unsalted butter, at room temperature

⅔ cup confectioners' sugar

¼ teaspoon vanilla extract

1 teaspoon orange zest (from about ½ large orange)

TO MAKE THE CINNAMON ROLLS:

1. Trace an 8-inch circle onto a piece of parchment paper. Cut out the circle and set aside.

2. On a lightly floured surface, roll out the thawed bread dough into a 7 x 5-inch rectangle. Brush the melted butter over the dough.

3. In a small bowl, stir together the brown sugar and ground cinnamon to combine. Sprinkle the cinnamon sugar over the dough, leaving a 1-inch border. Roll the dough tightly into a log. Cut the log into 4 equally sized rolls, about 1-inch thick.

4. Turn the rolls on their sides and cover with a kitchen towel. Let the dough rise in a warm environment for 1½ to 2 hours.

5. Once the rolls have risen, preheat your air fryer to 350°F for 10 minutes.

6. Using an oven mitt, carefully place the prepared parchment circle into the air fryer basket and place the cinnamon rolls into the air fryer basket. Bake the rolls for 5 minutes, rotate 180 degrees to ensure even browning, and continue baking for 4 minutes.

7. Make the cream cheese glaze while the rolls are baking: In a medium bowl, mix the cream cheese and butter to incorporate using either an electric hand-held mixer or a fork. Gradually add the confectioners' sugar and stir to combine. Add the vanilla extract and orange zest, and stir again to combine.

8. Remove the rolls from the air fryer and let cool slightly on a cooling rack. Drizzle cream cheese glaze over the rolls and serve warm.

Conversions

VOLUME CONVERSIONS		
U.S.	U.S. EQUIVALENT	METRIC
1 tablespoon (3 teaspoons)	½ fluid ounce	15 milliliters
¼ cup	2 fluid ounces	60 milliliters
⅓ cup	3 fluid ounces	90 milliliters
½ cup	4 fluid ounces	120 milliliters
⅔ cup	5 fluid ounces	150 milliliters
¾ cup	6 fluid ounces	180 milliliters
1 cup	8 fluid ounces	240 milliliters
2 cups	16 fluid ounces	480 milliliters

TEMPERATURE CONVERSIONS	
FAHRENHEIT (°F)	CELSIUS (°C)
125°F	50°C
150°F	65°C
175°F	80°C
200°F	95°C
225°F	110°C
250°F	120°C
275°F	135°C
300°F	150°C
325°F	165°C
350°F	175°C
375°F	190°C
400°F	200°C
425°F	220°C
450°F	230°C

WEIGHT CONVERSIONS	
U.S.	METRIC
½ ounce	15 grams
1 ounce	30 grams
2 ounces	60 grams
¼ pound	115 grams
⅓ pound	150 grams
½ pound	225 grams
¾ pound	350 grams
1 pound	450 grams

Recipe Index

Acknowledgments

I have been writing for my entire life, and I have been baking for about half of my life. I had my thirty-third birthday near the tail end of finishing this cookbook, and I do feel like I've learned a lot about myself. I have learned which flavors and ingredients I value the most (ground cinnamon, stone fruits, brown butter, a salty component in a sweet dessert). I've learned that I'm actually great with pastry. And I've learned how, exactly, baking can invoke a sense of real confidence. To Matt, for believing in me before I did, for being my baking guinea pig, for everything. To my family for instilling in me the importance of cooking and sitting down to eat a meal; of believing in the gift of sharing food. To my mom, for teaching me how to bake each year at Christmas, for your patience. To Bridget and the journalist Facebook group where I first heard about this project, thank you taking a chance on me. To Whiskey and Ginger cats, for always being so interested in what I'm doing in the kitchen; for being the best cats I've ever known. To my friends on Peach, for the input you'd give me when I'd crowdsource flavor combinations and other ideas for this project; for your friendship.

About the Author

Teresa Finney's food writing has appeared on Vice, Bravo!, *The Today Show*, *Civil Eats*, and elsewhere. Originally from the Bay Area, California, she studied English Literature in New York before moving to Atlanta, Georgia, to work as a recipe developer. Finney's passion is using the classic Mexican flavors she grew up on in baking projects. Visit her website www.milagrokitchen.com, or follow her on Twitter at @teresaafinney.

Printed in Great Britain
by Amazon

36945386R00116